A Birdke[illegible] Guide to

P[illegible] &
[illegible]aws

An invaluable guide to keeping and breeding a wide range of New World, African and Asian parrots

David Alderton

PUBLISHED BY
SALAMANDER BOOKS LIMITED
LONDON

A Salamander Book

ISBN 0 86101 990 3

All correspondence concerning the content of this volume should be addressed to Interpet Ltd.

Author

David Alderton has kept and bred a wide variety of birds for more than thirty years. He has travelled extensively in pursuit of this interest, visiting other enthusiasts in various parts of the world, including the United States, Canada and Australia. He has previously written a number of books on avicultural subjects, and contributes regularly to general and specialist publications in the UK and overseas. David studied veterinary medicine at Cambridge University, and now, in addition to writing, runs a highly respected international service that offers advice on the needs of animals kept in both domestic and commercial environments. He is also a Council Member of the Avicultural Society.

Photographer

Cyril Laubscher has been interested in aviculture and ornithology for more than thirty years and has travelled extensively in Europe, Australia and Southern Africa photographing wildlife. When he left England for Australia in 1966 as an enthusiastic aviculturalist, this fascination found expression as he began to portray birds photographically. In Australia he met the well-known aviculturalist Stan Sindel and, as a result of this association, seventeen of Cyril's photographs were published in Joseph Forshaw's original book on Australian Parrots in 1969. Since then, his photographs have met with considerable acclaim and the majority of those that appear here were taken specially for this book.

Credits

Editor: Anne McDowall
Design: Stuart Watkinson and Suzanne Baker
Colour reproductions: Bantam Litho Ltd.
Filmset: Flairplan Phototypesetting Ltd.
Printed in China

Contents

Introduction 6

Choosing parrots and macaws 8

Keeping parrots and macaws in the home 16

Keeping parrots and macaws in the garden 26

Feeding parrots and macaws 36

Basic health care 42

Breeding and rearing parrots and macaws 50

Species section 60

Index 94

Further reading 95

Picture credits 95

Above: *A pair of Black-headed Caiques*
Overleaf: *A pair of Celestial Parrotlets*

Introduction

Most people, even if they have no interest in birds, will recognize a parrot without difficulty. The reasons for their popularity as pets are obvious. Although some species are very expensive, noisy and destructive, most are quite easy to maintain, and few other pets will become as responsive to their owners. In addition, their potentially long lifespan is almost legendary; some are known to have lived for nearly a hundred years and most species will breed well into their twenties.

The 300 or so different parrot species are found mainly in the tropical areas of the world, where they have been kept as pets for centuries. In Central America, for example, it is clear from archaeological evidence that macaws and other parrots were being kept and bred successfully in aviary surroundings as long ago as the 1400s. It was at about this time, too, that parrots were introduced to Europe, where they soon became very popular as

companion birds. (King Henry VIII is just one monarch known to have owned a pet parrot, which possessed a large vocabulary.)

Until comparatively recently, most parrots were kept as pet birds, with relatively little emphasis being placed on breeding them. Since the early 1980s, however, there have been several significant changes in the way that parrots are kept, as knowledge about their nutritional and reproductive needs has advanced. This has meant that of about 280 species known to have been kept in captivity, at least 250 have bred successfully.

This book concentrates on the New World or neotropical species, from the diminutive parrotlets to the majestic macaws, which, at up to 1m(40in) long, are the largest members of the parrot group. Several African species, including the popular Grey Parrot, reckoned to be the most talented mimic of all species, are also included, along with two popular parrots from Asia.

Choosing parrots and macaws

The parrots and macaws covered in the latter section of this book (beginning on page 60) have a wide range of requirements, which you will need to consider carefully before deciding which species to buy. Here we look at general points you will need to consider, irrespective of the species you decide on, and whether you are buying a single pet or breeding stock for an aviary. You will need to think about your source of supply and, having found a good one that stocks the species you are looking for, you should examine any birds that interest you to ensure that they are healthy. (The checklist on page 15 provides a useful summary of what to look for.)

Finding a supplier

Check with the pet stores in your area to find which stock parrots. A number now purchase captive-bred, hand-raised birds from breeders and, depending on where you live, you should find a good choice of species available. A hand-raised parrot should not be nervous of people, as it will be naturally tame. It should readily perch on your hand and will be used to the sound of human voices. Such a bird will be easy to tame and you can expect it to develop into an effective mimic before long; some young parrots are starting to speak almost as soon as they are feeding themselves.

Alternatively, you may need to contact a specialist bird farm or breeder, many of whom advertize in the various birdkeeping publications. As a starting point, you can ask your newsagent about the availability of such magazines and then follow up with telephone calls to the advertizers located in your area. (You should always make an appointment to view the parrots they have on offer before deciding to buy). Most of the birds covered in this book are quite widely represented in collections in Europe and North America but, in some cases, you may have to be patient, or travel a distance, to obtain the bird of your choice.

Travelling boxes

Always take a suitable travelling box with you when you are planning to purchase a parrot. A box will provide a more suitable carrying container than a cage and, as it will cut out the light, it will be

Below: *Some species make better pets than others. The Grey Parrot is a popular pet bird and is renowned as a talented mimic.*

Above: *You will need a secure carrying container for transporting your parrot. A cat basket like this one is ideal. Never leave a bird alone in the car, where it will be vulnerable to heat stroke.*

less disturbing for the parrot. A bird will often cling onto the sides of a cage, and can damage its tail feathers as a result.

The most suitable type of container will depend to a large extent on the size of the bird, but wooden boxes are always preferable to cardboard ones. Even parrotlets can gnaw their way out of a cardboard container by enlarging the ventilation holes.

You can make a suitable carrying box from plywood, with a sliding hatch on top and ventilation holes around the sides. Position these holes fairly near the roof of the container, where they will be less accessible to the birds. As larger parrots are very adept at using their beaks to find any weakness in such a box, and may well be able to slide the hatch open, a hasp and padlock can be useful to ensure that the lid remains firmly closed.

If you are planning to keep only a single pet parrot, you may prefer to buy a suitable travelling box rather than make one yourself; many avicultural suppliers will be able to sell you one. Once you have brought your new companion home, keep the box safely, as you may need it again at a later date to take the parrot to a veterinarian.

Larger parrots, such as amazons, may feel more at home in an enclosed cat basket with a wire mesh grill at the front. Avoid wicker baskets of this type, however, as they will be no match for the birds' beaks. (If you have used the basket previously for your cat, you will also need to disinfect it thoroughly before placing the bird inside, as some bacteria normally associated with cats could also prove harmful to your parrot.)

Choosing a healthy bird

The vendor may offer to send you the parrot, but, if at all possible, you should collect the bird yourself. This gives you the opportunity to see the parrot's previous surroundings, and ask any questions about the diet and general care that your parrot has been receiving. Especially in the case of a young bird, be sure to ask for a diet sheet, and follow this closely for the first week or so. This should help to prevent any digestive upsets during its first few critical days with you.

Incidentally, never be tempted to purchase a young parrot that has been raised by hand and is not yet independent. Especially if you are not used to hand-feeding birds, this can prove, at the very least, a worrying period, and more serious complications do arise on occasions. You would be well advised to wait for a further few weeks, until your chosen youngster is fully independent.

Some breeders now sell their birds complete with a veterinary certificate of health. This may give you a safeguard when buying a young parrot, some of which are far more costly than a pedigree dog, but such a certificate provides no absolute guarantee of health and, even though a reputable breeder will not sell a chick unless he or she is certain that it is in top condition, you should always observe the bird carefully yourself.

Start by looking at the plumage. Most young parrots are duller in overall coloration than adults and their plumage may not be as sleek. Furthermore, especially around the mouth, deposits of food may have stuck the feathers together. To some extent, this is unavoidable, particularly as chicks at the weaning stage are likely to toy with the food on offer, rather than swallowing it. But if the plumage is fluffed up, and the parrot appears dull, then it could be ill. With older birds, beware of any patches of thin, grey downy feathers. This is

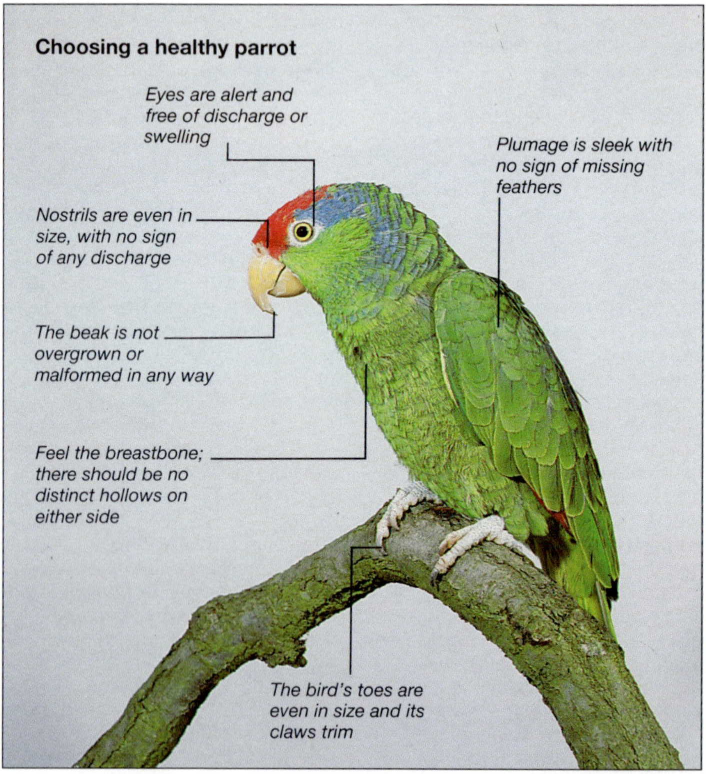

Below: *This Green-cheeked Amazon is in excellent condition. Regular bathing will help to keep the plumage sleek and attractive.*

Above: *This Eclectus hen shows severe signs of feather-plucking. The causes of this abnormal behaviour are varied.*

usually indicative of feather-plucking, which is a very difficult problem to eliminate, as it rapidly becomes habitual.

You will also need to look carefully at the nostrils to check that they are not blocked. A blocked nostril can lead to noisy breathing, and may be indicative of a minor respiratory infection. If left untreated over a period of years, the affected nostril may become enlarged and misshapen.

The eyes, too, should be clear from any sign of discharge. A healthy parrot will be alert and will keep its eyes open when you are nearby. Check for any swelling around the eyes; especially in young imported parrots, this could be an indication of a more serious problem, or simply the result of a Vitamin A deficiency.

Look closely at the feet. Parrots normally perch with two toes gripping the front of the perch and two providing support behind. On occasions, especially if they have been kept on a slippery surface or unsuitable bedding during the rearing period, one toe may have slipped forward. This problem, sometimes described as 'slipped toe', will be virtually impossible to correct in a weaned youngster and the bird will be handicapped to some extent throughout its life. This need not prevent it settling well as a pet, however. Over a period of time, it should normally adapt to its situation, but you will almost certainly need to trim the nail of the affected toe at regular intervals as, not being subjected to normal wear, it will become overgrown.

Another disorder, more commonly associated with hand-raised than with aviary-bred parrots, is swollen toes. You are most likely to encounter this in Grey and Eclectus Parrots. The precise cause is unclear; it may well be a local infection, although some people believe that there could be a nutritional link as well, in the form of a shortage of Vitamin B in the rearing formula.

The toes of a young parrot should be of a similar width. Sometimes swelling is apparent close to the nail of one or more digits. Affected birds show no apparent signs of discomfort, and seem to be healthy in other respects. However, the swelling usually interferes with the blood supply to the toes, causing gangrene, so that the lower part of the digit, including the nail, is lost. This takes place over several weeks, shrivelling up before breaking off, with little, if any, blood loss. Further problems are unlikely, and the stub should heal rapidly.

These various disorders are uncommon, but you should be aware of them when assessing a young parrot before deciding whether or not to buy. Finally, with the vendor's permission, see if you can persuade the bird to step onto your hand. Wear a glove; youngsters have quite sharp claws. So as not to frighten the bird, move slowly, raising your hand towards the perch. It may then step readily onto your outstretched fingers. Do not worry if it is reluctant, so long as you are certain it is a young bird. Many parrots are rather suspicious of the close presence of strangers, although they are very tame with people they know well.

Choosing pet birds

If you are seeking a pet parrot, it is vital to choose a young bird, which should settle well in your home. Older individuals will be much harder to tame successfully, and rarely prove to be talented talkers.

You could also consider buying an established pet, which is already tame and talking. However, although this may appear the most satisfactory option, it can be less rewarding in practice, because of the natural instincts of most parrots. These birds generally live in flocks or small groups, with individual members or pairs maintaining a strong bond between each other. A pet parrot comes to identify closely with its owner as a substitute partner and it can therefore be difficult to persuade a tame bird to settle well in new surroundings. The adjustment may take months, and mature birds may even resort to feather-plucking when transferred to a new home.

It can be especially difficult to integrate a pet parrot that has spent several years living in a store into domestic surroundings. Having been used to the constant stream of people and attention in a shop, where it may have been the focal point, such birds often pine when first introduced to the relative tranquillity of a home with an unfamiliar owner. (Of course, this will apply only to parrots that have been kept as the focal point of the store, not to those that have been kept for sale for only a short time.)

Owning a pet parrot can be a life-long commitment, so do not be seduced by the cuddly appearance of a youngster. Hand-raised birds need a great deal of attention, and if you suspect that you could be away from home for much of the day, do seriously consider obtaining two birds. They will provide company for each other (irrespective of their gender), and there is no reason why both should not develop into tame, talking companions. In addition, if you think that you may want to breed parrots at a later stage, you will do better to start off with a young pair, than to try to pair up a single pet bird later in life.

Attempting to introduce a companion to an established pet can be very difficult; the newcomer is likely to arouse jealousy in your bird, and even overt aggression. In view of the sharp beaks of most parrots, it can be very dangerous to place unfamiliar birds together in the confines of a cage when one is already well settled as a member of the family.

If you select two young birds from the outset, they will grow up as equals, sharing your attention, and there is unlikely to be any serious friction. However, some amazon cocks can become aggressive for a period while in breeding condition, and may turn on their partners. Separating the birds for a while should hopefully solve the problem.

Choosing breeding stock

If you are buying parrots to breed, you will have a greater range of options available and will not be tied to obtaining recently fledged

Below: *It is a good idea to wear a glove when training your parrot, or it may inflict a painful bite.*

Above: *Macaws make great companions, but avoid buying a bird kept as a shop pet, as it will be used to constant attention.*

birds. Once a parrot is in mature plumage, it will be difficult to age unless it has been captive-bred and is close-rung (that is, it has a continuous circular band on its leg, indicating, among other things, its year of birth). You may sometimes be able to recognize young adults, however, particularly in the case of certain of the larger species. The eye coloration of Grey Parrots (see page 91), for example, may take several years to become truly straw-yellow. Plumage changes may take place over the course of several moults, most notably in the case of the Double Yellow-headed Amazon (see page 66), where the area of yellow plumage increases to cover the head, replacing the green fledging plumage, over a period of four years or so.

The precise age of the parrot is not necessarily significant, in view of the long reproductive life of these larger parrots, but it can be reassuring to know that your chosen bird is quite young, as breeding stock is expensive.

Pet shops may not have breeding stock available, so you may have to follow up advertisements from private breeders. Try to establish the reason for the sale if at all possible. Although proven pairs usually command a premium price, they can be a good investment, simply because you know the birds are compatible.

Particularly with the larger species, it is, unfortunately, not sufficient simply to house a cock and hen together, provide ideal surroundings, and wait for the chicks! In some cases, it appears, the pair in question just do not take to each other. This has become clearly apparent during recent years with the establishment of large-scale breeding units, where birds are housed and fed under identical and optimum conditions. Changing partners can result in almost instantaneous nesting if all other factors are suitable.

The ideal, though expensive, solution when choosing breeding pairs of the larger parrots, such as amazons, macaws and the Grey

Parrot, is to purchase a number of individuals; at least four, and preferably six. House them all together in a large aviary and observe them carefully to see which birds are compatible with each other. You can then transfer the pair to separate breeding accommodation.

The advent of reliable sexing methods means that you can start with, say, three apparent pairs, even if not all the birds prove to be compatible. At a dealer's premises, where unsexed birds may be housed together in a group, you will have to rely on behavioural observation. Watch them closely, and you should come to recognize pair-bonded individuals.

You may notice that two birds in a group tend to follow each other, remaining in close contact as they move around. At times, they will pause to preen their partner's head and neck, and they are also likely to roost together. However, you may lose sight of the pair when the dealer tries to catch the birds for you, unless you can clearly distinguish them.

The subject of compatibility has not been well studied to date, but it appears to be a more significant influence in determining breeding success in some species than was previously thought. In a few cases, with larger psittacines, such as the Eclectus and Great-billed Parrot (see pages 92-3), the pair bond appears much more tenuous, and so these species are far less choosy about their mate.

Above: *Most amazons are not sexually dimorphic, and you will therefore need to buy reliably sexed birds if you want to start with a potential breeding pair.*

It seems likely that where pair-bonding does occur, it takes place around the time of maturity, usually when the parrots are approaching four years old. Clearly, if two birds have been kept together up to this stage, then they are likely to accept each other as mates. It may therefore be worth purchasing aviary-bred or even hand-raised chicks for breeding purposes. Although this may seem a lengthy process, there are several advantages; you should end up with a bonded pair, which, hopefully, will breed consistently for a decade or more, and you will know their ages and past history. (If you start with imported birds, you can be certain of none of these points and the change of environment means that they may take three years or more to become established in their new quarters, which is as long as a pair of youngsters may take to mature.)

In addition to these advantages, you will find that young birds are easier to manage than recently imported stock if you have no previous experience. Despite the fact that they are likely to be more expensive, a sexed pair of young parrots could well prove a better long-term proposition.

Try to obtain the young birds from different sources, so that you can be certain they are unrelated. Sibling pairings allow less genetic diversity in the resulting chicks than any other, and so will potentially harm any attempts to develop a strain over a period of time. This applies especially to the more prolific psittacines, such as the small parrotlets. It is also much better to be able to offer unrelated pairs once you yourself have surplus stock. You should work, therefore, with a minimum of two original pairs.

When you are contemplating buying breeding birds for an aviary, always ask where they are presently being housed. Bear in mind that you should transfer neither hand-raised youngsters nor recently imported parrots to an outdoor aviary during the winter months in temperate climates. It is better to acquire such parrots in the late spring, when the weather is turning mild, to avoid the need to prepare temporary accommodation for them over the colder months.

Choosing parrots and macaws

Parrotlets	The small size of these quiet birds makes them easy to accommodate in an aviary. Pairs generally need to be kept apart as they will fight if housed in adjoining aviaries without adequate double-wiring.
Amazon and pionus parrots	Amazons are particularly vocal in the early morning and evening. They are intelligent birds and youngsters can prove good mimics.
Vasa parrots	These recent introductions to aviculture should not be kept as pets in the home.
Macaws	Tame birds can form a very strong bond with their owners, but accommodation for the large species can be a problem. Feather-plucking can be the result of boredom, a poor diet, sexual frustration or a lack of bathing facilities.
Grey Parrot *Poicephalus* parrots	Young Greys settle well as pets, and prove talented mimics, as may *Poicephalus* parrots. Untame adults are nervous in comparison, and need to be housed in aviaries. Both groups are relatively quiet. Greys are also susceptible to feather-plucking. Check weight of *Poicephalus* parrots, as they lose condition quite rapidly.
Eclectus and Great-billed Parrots	Eclectus often breed through much of the year. Relatively little is known about Greatbills. Newly imported birds of both species are often in poor feather condition and need careful management.

Keeping parrots and macaws in the home

Parrots that are typically kept as pets also tend to be the most destructive members of the group. It has been calculated that a large macaw, for example, can exert a pressure of 300 p.s.i. with its beak.

Here, we look at how to provide suitable accommodation for a pet parrot, and how to tame it, so that it becomes a life-long companion.

Choosing a suitable flight

Most importantly, don't try to economize on the size or the design of housing for your bird. Although a baby macaw purchased as a pet may appear a rather innocent bundle of feathers, it will soon develop into a robust adolescent bird, eager to exercise both its wings and beak. If frustrated in its attempts, it is likely to end up plucking its feathers, or calling loudly for long periods.

Whereas parrotlets can be accommodated quite satisfactorily in units intended for budgerigars, macaws and amazons, in particular, require a much larger and more robust structure. The gauge of the mesh is important – thick 12G (gauge) is ideal for the large macaws, although thinner mesh, up to 16G, may be satisfactory. The size of mesh is also important; a macaw will be able to slip its beak easily through mesh that is more than 2.5cm(1in) square, gaining leverage and exerting great pressure on the individual strands. Parrots often do not break through mesh at the first

An indoor flight cage for a macaw

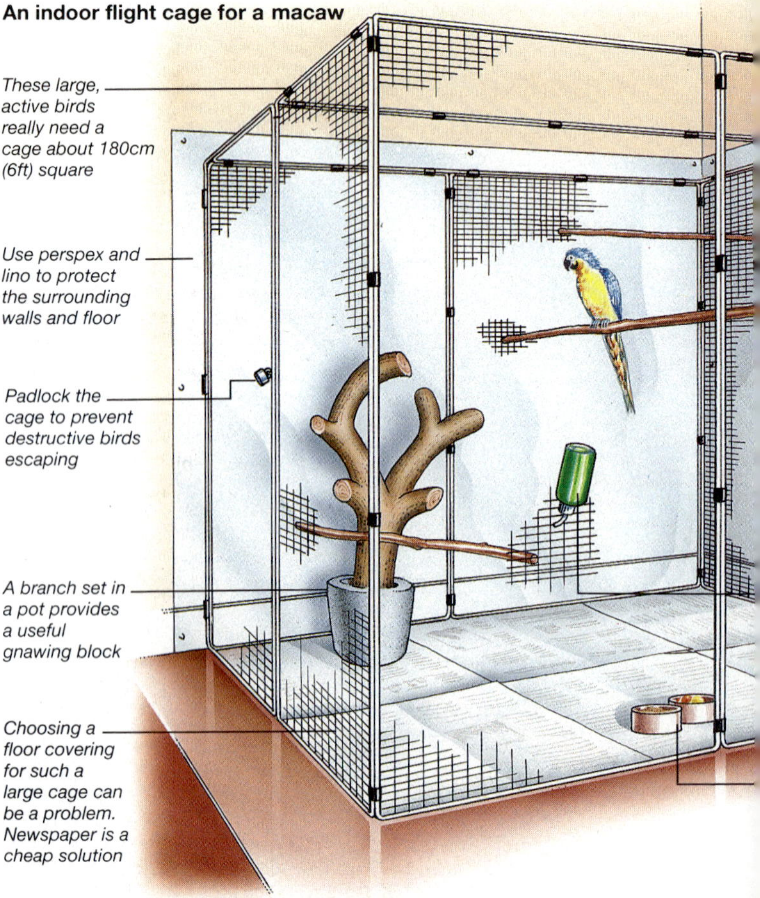

attempt, but play with the strands, bending them back and forth with their powerful beaks and muscular tongues. Over a period of time, this weakens the mesh, which will eventually snap, and the sharp ends can then easily injure the parrot's tongue. If the bird swallows a small piece, this may impact in the wall of the gizzard, or elsewhere in the digestive tract, with potentially fatal consequences.

The traditional square design of many parrot cages is really unsuitable for the active nature of parrots, allowing them very little space for exercise, and circular cages are even less satisfactory. Fortunately, a wide range of housing options is now available.

Rather than buy a rigid design, you can plan the bird's accommodation yourself, using flexible panel systems. Ready-to-assemble panels are produced in standard sizes, and you can select the number of panels you require to make a chosen design. Separate door units are also available. These panels are made of mesh fixed to a metal framework, which is more durable than timber. Although the finish is usually very good, you should check that there are no sharp pieces of galvanized metal present, which could be dangerous. Parrots often climb around their quarters, and if one of these splinters penetrates a bird's fleshy tongue, it will not only be painful, but may also result in serious blood loss.

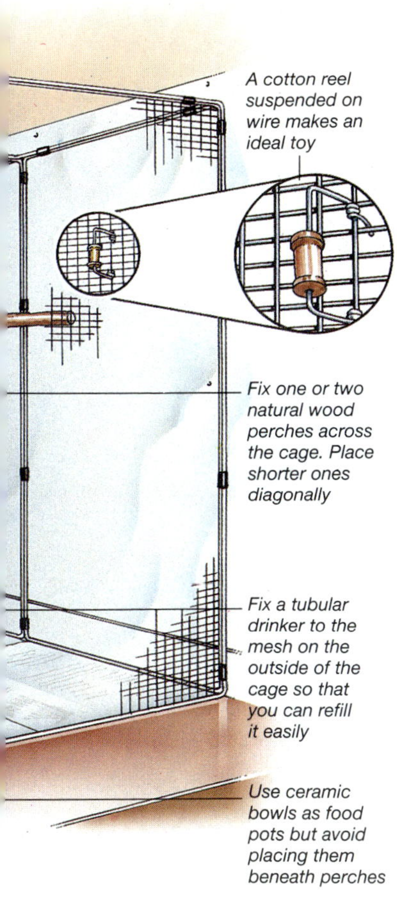

Easy access to the inside of the flight unit is important for cleaning and feeding purposes. Unfortunately, some designs do not incorporate a sliding tray in the base and it is not always possible to purchase a suitable tray to correspond to the dimensions of the flight. This means that in order to clean the floor properly, you will need to lift the whole of the flight unit off the base. Apart from being quite heavy, the unit will also be cumbersome in a confined space.

A mesh floor, made of the same panels as the side and roof of the flight, is the obvious solution, but you will have to use paper as the floor covering (rather than bird sand, for example) and parrots are likely to shred this. You can place the paper beneath the cage, where it will be out of the parrot's reach, but the mesh will then become soiled from above. As well as changing the paper regularly, you will also have to detach the mesh and scrub it frequently to remove the droppings.

The best solution may be to make a base to fit the dimensions of your flight. Allow a gap of at least 2.5cm(1in) between the bottom of the flight and the base unit to insert a separate sliding tray. If you decide to use metal sheeting, rather than timber with a plywood tray, you must ensure that there are

Above: *If you choose a standard cage, make sure it is large enough and that the bars are horizontal, so the parrot can climb around.*

no sharp edges on which the parrot could slice its toes. You should also check the corners carefully for any gaps in which the bird's claw could become caught.

If you come to the conclusion that the problem of cleaning a panel-system flight outweighs the advantages of its versatility and low cost, you may decide to choose a ready-made indoor flight unit that comes complete with a base. Several stylish designs are available, but you should make sure that the model you choose is sufficiently robust for the species you want to keep.

Perches

You can help to deflect your parrot's attention from its quarters by providing an adequate supply of branches as perches. Never use plastic perches, even if these are supplied with the unit. Although easy to clean, they appear to cause birds discomfort, and your parrot will be reluctant to use them. Some birdkeepers use dowelling of the appropriate size, but undoubtedly the best option is to provide fresh-cut branches. The required diameter depends to some extent on the size of the bird, although some variation is desirable, as this exercises the toes. (This is one reason for avoiding dowelling, which is of a constant diameter.) Perches should be sufficiently thick to enable the parrot to grip well, without its front and rear toes coming into contact with each other beneath the perch.

You can choose branches for perches from a variety of trees and shrubs but, bearing in mind that parrots frequently swallow some of the wood, you should avoid any poisonous plants, such as lilac (*Syringa*), yew (*Taxus*) and laburnum (*Laburnum*). You may have access to fruit trees, but don't use any that may have been recently sprayed with chemicals in case the residues prove harmful.

Wash all branches thoroughly, before placing them in the parrot's quarters, to remove any droppings of wild birds or excessive algal growth. Use clean water and a scrubbing brush for this purpose,

Below: *Parrots are destructive birds by nature, but by gnawing on wood, they keep their beaks in trim and prevent them overgrowing.*

avoiding detergent or disinfectant, which, again, may prove to be poisonous.

Dead branches may be easier to acquire, but are not recommended as they are likely to be a source of fungal spores, which could harm your parrot. In addition, dried wood is more likely to split as it is gnawed. The fleshy cheek patches of macaws are vulnerable to sharp splinters, which may become lodged here from inside the mouth. Although not a common problem, this does arise on occasions, with a pronounced swelling appearing where the splinter entered the flesh.

Arrange the perches across the flight rather than along its length to give the parrot greater opportunity for exercise. Do not position them so that they overhang each other, or the lower perches will be soiled with droppings from above, and avoid fixing the perches too close to the ends of the flight, or the parrot's tail may be damaged where it rubs on the mesh.

Most parrots start to gnaw their branches from the ends. If you cut the perch so that it is just wider than the flight, and fix it at a slight angle, you should not have to replace it too frequently, as you can simply slide it into a straighter position later, when the parrots have worn it down. Once it becomes too short to fit across the width of the flight, you may be able to place the perch diagonally at one end where it will provide a valuable gnawing block for the parrots.

In a cage for parrotlets, you can simply notch the perches so that they fit tidily into the mesh, but with other parrots, you will need to secure them more firmly. Twist a stout strand of wire around each end of the perch, loop it through the mesh and secure firmly in place on the outside of the flight, keeping the cut ends out of the birds' reach.

Toys

It is important to provide some basic toys for a pet parrot living on its own. Do not be tempted to offer the plastic toys sold for budgerigars, however. A parrot will destroy these quite easily and there may also be sharp metal projections inside such toys that would be out of reach of a less destructive bird.

Toys suitable for parrots are

Below: *Toys will occupy pet parrots and prevent boredom and feather-plucking. Suitable ones need to be simple, safe, and robust.*

generally hard to find, but it is not difficult to improvize. A popular toy with many birds is a clean cotton reel (with its labels removed), suspended on a strand of wire coat-hanger, so that it can be slid up and down by the bird. You will be able to replace the reel easily once the parrot has gnawed it away. A mirror placed at perch level outside the cage can provide companionship for the parrot when you are out, as will a radio.

Many parrots appear to derive most pleasure from gnawing their perches. They will start by removing any loose branches and stripping the bark, before progressing to destroy the perch itself. Never be tempted to replace a wooden perch with an indestructible item, such as a metal rod, even if you need to replace branches two or three times weekly. You will probably notice that your bird's interest in attacking the wood tends to vary through the year; parrots entering breeding condition will be especially destructive. The parrot's beak will become overgrown if you provide nothing on which it can gnaw, and you may eventually have to cut it back to enable the bird to eat.

Positioning the flight unit

If you choose a flight unit that is mounted on castors, you will be able to move your pet about more easily. You will, nevertheless, need to find an area where the unit can be kept most of the time. Choose a position out of direct sunlight; although most parrots are tropical birds, they can die rapidly from the effects of heat stroke. Especially in the early stages, the parrot will need a spot where it feels secure. A corner of a room is a good place, as the parrot can withdraw to the back of the flight if it feels threatened.

It is advisable to protect the walls, since parrots tend to be messy feeders, and may also pass droppings onto the wall as they climb around their quarters. Some kind of curtaining that can be easily cleaned is most satisfactory. If necessary, you can, of course, use polythene sheeting, although its appearance is obviously less attractive. You will need to ensure that the hanging curtains or polythene are out of reach of the parrot, otherwise the bird will be encouraged to hold onto the sides of the flight, in an attempt to reach the protective material behind. You may also want to place a rug on the

Positioning the flight unit

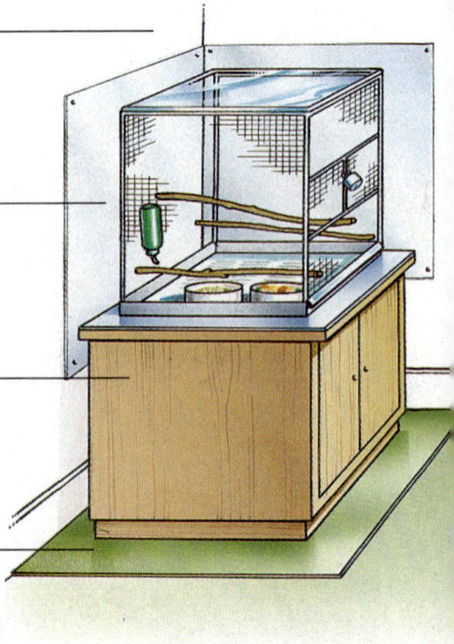

A site in a corner of the room should help your parrot to settle and to feel secure. If possible, avoid placing the unit directly against a shared wall.

Protect the walls with sheets of perspex or old curtains. You can also cover the top of the cage with perspex to deter a pet cat from sitting here.

A sturdy piece of furniture makes a good base for a smaller cage, such as this. A taller flight will be easy to move if it is mounted on castors.

Place a piece of linoleum or a rug beneath the cage, extending about 30cm (1ft) around its edges, to protect the carpet from husks and droppings.

floor to protect the carpet. This should extend about 30cm(1ft) around the edges of the flight unit.

Because of the amount of noise a parrot can make, it is best to avoid placing the flight unit directly against a shared wall, if possible. Amazon parrots, in particular, often have regular periods of screeching during the early morning and evening and, while this might not disturb you, your neighbour may not share your enthusiasm!

If you keep a cat, you will need to take particular care when introducing a parrot to your household. Choose a flight with mesh not more than 2.5cm(1in) square or the cat may be able to reach inside the flight with its paws.

It is not only the parrot that could be in danger, however; should the cat strike and miss, there is a possibility that the parrot may retaliate and bite the cat's leg. A cat sitting on the roof of the bird's quarters presents the greatest danger, and you may want to add a false roof of solid plastic to deter any confrontation.

Some cats prove more interested in pet parrots than others, and although you should never relax your guard entirely, a state of semi-harmony can be reached. Be careful, however, not to show too much overt affection to another pet in the presence of your parrot as this can give rise to jealousy, with the bird screaming loudly for attention. This situation is more prone to occur if you add to your collection of animals after obtaining a parrot; the parrot will usually grow to tolerate established pets in time.

The early days

Try to set up everything at home before you obtain your parrot, so that you can transfer it straight to its new quarters without delay. Place food close to a perch, because in unfamiliar surroundings, many birds are reluctant to feed on the floor. Water, too, should be within easy reach. If it is dark when you reach home, leave a room light on for an hour or so, to allow the parrot to settle down.

Some owners like to cover their parrot at night so that the bird is not exposed to abnormally long periods of light, which may interfere with the moulting cycle. If you decide to adopt this practice, you will need a thick cover, preferably of a non-woven fabric, so that the bird can not catch its claws in it and

Hazards in the home

Parrots do not always appreciate the presence of a pane of glass and it is therefore a good idea to cover windows with a curtain or blind to prevent your bird flying into them.

Some house plants may prove poisonous if your parrot eats them, and even those that are not may be destroyed. Ideally, you should remove them from the room.

Live or open-bar fires are obviously dangerous. Always unplug and, ideally, remove electrical appliances before letting your parrot out of its cage.

Although your pets may eventually learn to tolerate each other, it is wise to shut a cat out of the room while your parrot is out of its cage.

injure itself. There is no need to tie this in place; simply drape it over the roof and allow it to trail down the sides, leaving a slight gap for ventilation at the bottom.

Avoid disturbing a newly acquired parrot more than necessary for the first few days, to allow it time to settle in its new surroundings. Keep a close watch on its food and water intake, as well as its droppings. If you suspect anything is amiss, contact a veterinarian; early treatment can be vital in ensuring a recovery. (See *Basic health care*, pages 42–49.)

Taming your parrot

Within a few days, you can try offering the parrot slices of fruit by hand, in order to win its confidence. If it initially refuses to feed in this way, try again later, perhaps in the late afternoon, when parrots feed before retiring to roost for the night. A hand-raised bird will rarely refuse an offering, and may even beg for food, attracting your attention by head-bobbing and calling for food at the same time. Aviary-bred or imported youngsters may be more reticent, but you need not worry, provided that the young parrot is clearly eating on its own. In the wild, the young of certain species, such as the large macaws, stay with their parents in family groups for a considerable period and may still try to solicit food from an adult even after they are weaned.

Once the parrot is feeding readily from your hand, initially taking food pushed through the cage mesh, and then accepting it from your hand inside the flight, you will have started to win its confidence. You should then find it quite straightforward to persuade a hand-raised chick to step from the perch onto your hand or arm. If the bird is reluctant, you can try to bribe it by holding a piece of fruit or other favourite food item, such as a groundnut (a peanut in its shell) just out of the parrot's reach while it remains on the perch. Place your arm in front of the perch to encourage the bird to step onto it to reach the food item. As with all stages in training, keep repeating the procedure until the parrot is responding without hesitation. It should then allow you to stroke its head, indicating its request by tilting its head slightly to one side and ruffling its feathers. This is a clear sign of acceptance, which may not be extended to other members of the family.

Even if the parrot is really intended to be your pet, it is a good idea to encourage other people to be involved to some extent in its care, however. If you have to go away for any time, it will help if the parrot will accept someone else's attention in your absence. Nevertheless, they should be cautious; your pet is unlikely to be as trusting with anyone else, and may bite unexpectedly.

Below: *Although more expensive, young hand-raised parrots are more likely to become tame pets.*

Above: *A tame parrot, such as this White-bellied Caique, will allow its owner to stroke it.*

Teaching your parrot to talk

The length of time it takes to tame a parrot and teach it to talk varies considerably. Indeed, it may not even be possible to really tame an adult bird. Much depends, firstly, on how tame the parrot was when you acquired it, and, secondly, on how much time you can devote to the training process each day. Regular short spells of five to ten minutes during the day will be much more effective than a single lengthy session every weekend.

Most parrots find it easier to mimic the voices of women or children, although they often respond adequately to men as well, and some species prove more natural talkers than others. The Grey Parrot is universally accepted as the most talented member of the family in this regard, although most amazons can acquire a large vocabulary and have clear diction. Macaws are rather less able to build up an extensive repertoire, but can certainly be taught a few words. Pionus parrots and *Poicephalus* species can also prove able mimics, but they are less often kept as pets. There is even a record of a parrotlet being taught a few words successfully.

You will need to repeat a chosen word or phrase many times before the parrot will copy you. Start with something simple, such as 'Hello Joey', when you go into the room. The bird will soon come to associate this phrase with your presence, and should eventually respond by repeating it.

Build up the vocabulary carefully, so that the bird does not become confused. Bear in mind that it is difficult to persuade a parrot to drop words from its vocabulary once it has mastered them, though you could try covering the cage briefly when the bird uses it, in the hope that this may act as an effective deterrent.

Studies of talking parrots have suggested that, in some cases, the bird is able to associate a particular word with a request, so that it can learn to ask for 'fruit please', for example. You can build up a parrot's vocabulary over many years. They are capable of learning over 500 words, and you can even teach them songs by training them to repeat a line at a time.

In North America, especially, audio cassettes and CDs are now available to help with teaching your pet to talk, while videos can help with the training process itself. There is really no substitute to teaching your bird to talk directly, however, to maintain its interest, but it may be helpful to make your own recordings, so that you can play tapes of your own voice when you have to go out. This will provide company for your pet and will also reinforce its talking lessons in your absence.

Parrots will also pick up other sounds from their environment. Greys are especially talented whistlers, probably because their natural calls are comprised of a series of similar sounds. They may also learn how to imitate a barking dog, or even the sound of a ringing telephone. This can be particularly disorientating, so, if possible, try to keep your 'phone out of earshot of your bird, otherwise you may have difficulty distinguishing between a genuine call and your parrot!

Letting your parrot out of its cage
Once your bird is perching readily on your arm and has settled well in the home, you will have to decide whether or not you will let it venture out into the room. Generally, this is to be recommended, especially if you can devote a particular time every day, perhaps during the evening, to playing with your pet. These times will undoubtedly strengthen the bond between you, and the parrot will soon settle into the routine of coming out, and then returning to its quarters. Indeed, after an initial investigation, it may perch happily on a special stand for much of the evening.

Suitable stands are sometimes incorporated as part of a flight cage, being added above the outside roof, where parrots often feel most secure. Alternatively, many pet stores stock special stout wooden T-shaped stands with a food and water pot at either end and a tray beneath, to catch seed husks and droppings. Do not be tempted to acquire a leg chain for a parrot, especially if your bird is not tame. If it is frightened for any reason, it will try to fly off the perch, and is likely to be left dangling upside down from the chain.

Never leave a parrot loose in a room if you are not present. There are a number of potential dangers here (see page 21), including uncovered windows. Parrots do not always appreciate the presence of a solid barrier of glass, and may fly into a large pane.

Open or electric-bar fires are another hazard, as is a live

Above: *A secure stand is useful for a tame parrot, such as this Grey, providing it with a place to perch and feed while out of its cage.*

electrical flex. Macaws especially, can bite through a flex with devastating speed, and will receive a lethal shock from a live wire. Check that all appliances are switched off before you let the parrot out into the room.

Some house plants may prove poisonous if the parrot eats them, and flaking paintwork that contains lead will also represent a hazard.

Adequate supervision is also important to protect your furnishings; many pet parrots can inflict serious damage on wooden furniture with their powerful beaks, and can also wreck curtains. Until used to being let out, your bird may fly around wildly, knocking over ornaments and hurting itself.

Wing-clipping
With all the potential damage that a parrot could cause both itself and your home, you may decide, like many birdkeepers, to clip your parrot's wings. With its wings

clipped, the bird will still be able to fly, but with less power. Carried out properly, this procedure is quite painless, with no long-term effects; at the next moult (within a year), the cut feathers will be shed and replaced by a full set, enabling the parrot to fly again normally. (You may find, however, that your pet is rather withdrawn for a day or so afterwards, because of the indignity of being handled and restrained for this purpose.)

Even with a semi-tame parrot, it is sensible to wear a protective pair of gloves – ideally, a thin pair of gloves beneath gardening gauntlets – as the vice-like grip of the large macaws can be especially painful. Never wear knitted gloves of any kind when handling these birds, as their claws and beak may become caught up in the woollen strands, which, in any case, will offer you little protection.

Open the door of the cage and reach in to restrain the bird, using both hands to keep the wings closed and prevent the bird struggling. Take care not to frighten the parrot unnecessarily by making sudden movements. If you are right-handed, use your left hand, fingers pointing upwards, to restrain its wings, and then move your hand up so that you are holding the bird's head between your first and second fingers while the wings and back are covered in the palm of your hand. It is vital not to press on the sides of the neck, or you could prevent the parrot from breathing; your fingers should act as a restraint, not a clamp. With its head movements restricted, the parrot will be less able to bite you.

Try to find someone to help you clip your parrot's wings. With the larger species, especially, you really need one person to hold the bird, leaving the other free to concentrate on cutting the flight feathers. Open up one wing, and, with a sharp pair of scissors (preferably with round rather than pointed ends), cut across the flight feathers in a straight line, leaving the outer two intact. Do not cut below the start of the individual feather shafts, but leave a small amount of feathering at the top. There will then be no risk of bleeding, as this part of the feather is dead. When a new feather is growing, there is a blood supply within the shaft, and cutting the feather too short at this point will result in a haemorrhage.

While parrots are not generally disturbed by having their feathers clipped in this way, some tend to pull at the remaining bare shafts. They may do this instinctively, because once the stub of damaged feather is removed, another full feather will grow to replace it.

Clipping a parrot's wing
Hold the wing open and cut across the feathers as shown. Leave the outermost primary feathers intact.

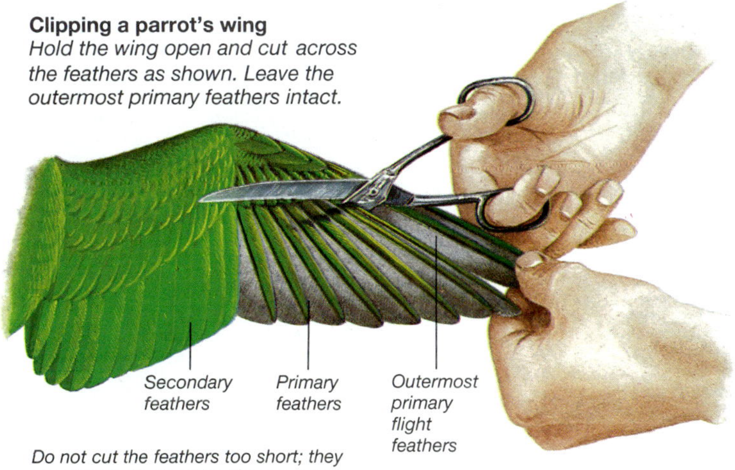

Do not cut the feathers too short; they may bleed. Seek advice if necessary.

Keeping parrots and macaws in the garden

Before planning an aviary for this group of birds, you will need to consider whether their calls are likely to cause offense to close neighbours. Some species, such as the parrotlets, lack the harsh screech of amazon parrots and the large macaws, and an aviary for these smaller birds will also prove far less costly than one for their larger relatives.

If you do want to keep amazons or macaws in the garden, you may be able to design suitable birdroom accommodation for them, and, with adequate sound-proofing, such an arrangement should be suitable even in a fairly suburban area. The parrots will breed without any problems in such surroundings; indeed, results can be better in a darkened environment, which offers greater seclusion.

The size of the aviary will obviously depend to an extent on the species you want to keep. Parrotlets will thrive in a relatively small area; an aviary with a 90cm(3ft) square shelter attached to a flight 180cm(6ft) long will suffice for a pair of these birds. Medium-sized and larger parrots, such as the Senegal and pionus species, will benefit from a flight at least 360cm(12ft) in length, and vasas, which are particularly strong fliers, will show to best effect in an even longer flight.

The width of the flight is less significant, especially since most parrots are kept in pairs, rather than on a colony system. A width of 90cm(3ft) will suffice for the smaller, short-tailed species, with 120cm(4ft) being adequate for most of the others, except the long-tailed macaws, for which a flight 180cm(6ft) wide is ideal.

In many cases, you will not need to make an official planning application in order to build an aviary, but do check on local regulations before beginning the work. Mistakes about the need for planning permission can be expensive if you have to dismantle a finished structure.

The standard aviary

Parrotlets are the easiest parrots to house, because they are not especially destructive to woodwork. A well-made budgerigar aviary, comprised of a flight with an attached shelter, will suit them quite adequately. Birdkeeping magazines carry advertisements offering both aviaries built to specific dimensions and kits, from which you can construct an aviary to your own design. The latter provides a more versatile option, especially if you want to build a small row of flights to accommodate several pairs.

Below: *A standard block of parrot aviaries. The flights are empty of any vegetation, as most parrots are destructive by nature and will soon attack any plants in their aviary. Partitions are double wired.*

Possible aviary plans

Below: *The size of aviary you decide on will depend to a large extent on the species you want to keep. Here are three layouts.*

A simple parrotlet aviary

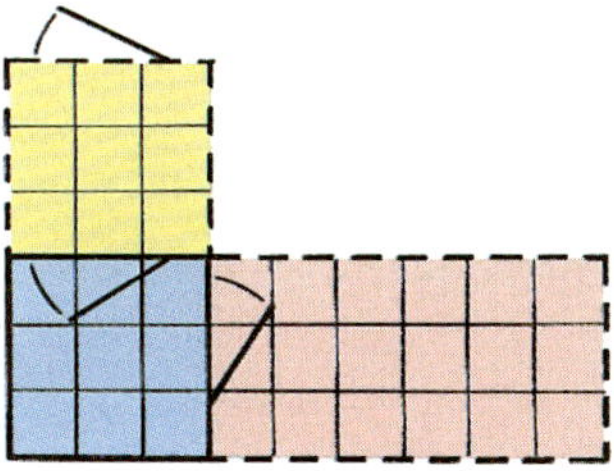

A standard double aviary

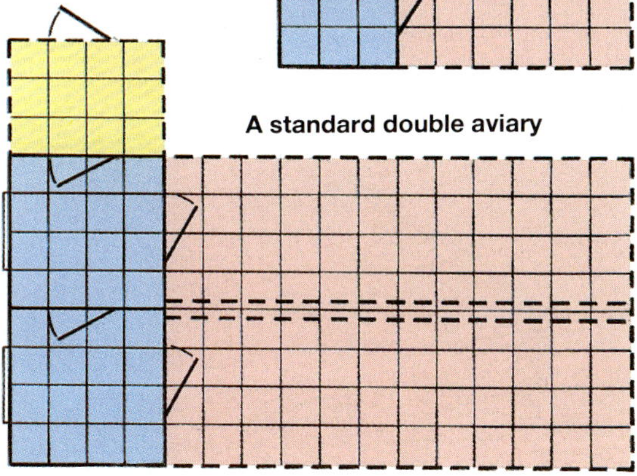

A large structure, with service corridor, suitable for large macaws

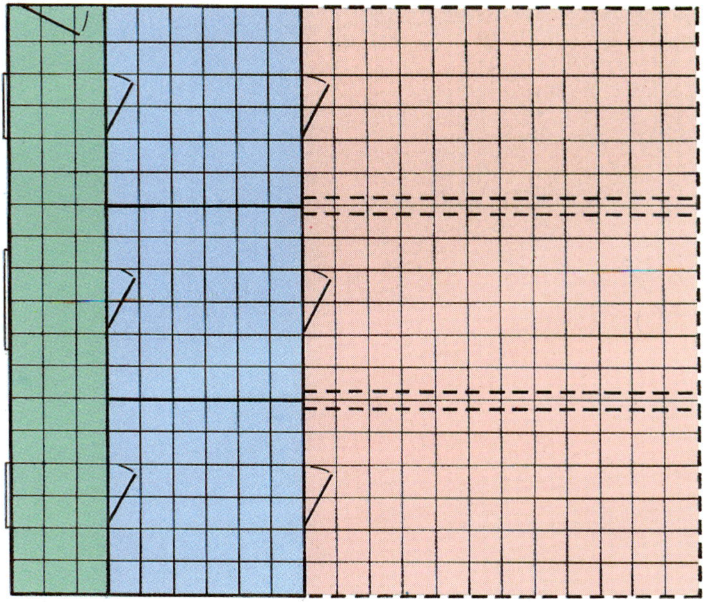

The flight panels should be constructed from timber that is at least 3.75cm(1.5in) square, preferably jointed. As aviary mesh is most commonly available in sheets 90cm(3ft) wide, flight panels are usually made at this size to avoid wastage. Check that the timber is safely weatherproofed (some companies charge extra for such treatment). Weatherproofing timber for outdoor use will greatly help to prolong its lifespan.

You may be offered a choice of mesh. For parrotlets, 19 gauge is adequate, and ideally, the dimensions should be 1.25cm(0.5in) square, although 2.5x1.25cm(1x0.5in), which is cheaper, should be adequate to exclude mice. The mesh should cover the inner face of the frame, to

The standard parrotlet aviary

prevent the birds reaching the woodwork. If you are planning to build a block of flights, check that both sides of connecting panels are wired, so that parrotlets in adjoining flights cannot injure each other's toes through the mesh. (It is, of course, possible to buy the timber, mesh and other materials separately and make your own flight, but, particularly if you want to build a block of aviaries, this is rarely economic.)

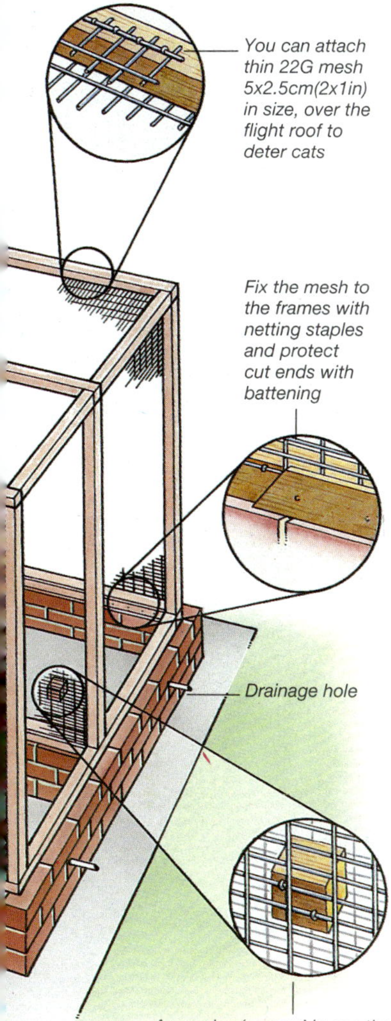

Where you position the entrance may depend on where you propose to site the aviary in the garden, but you can place a door into either the flight or the shelter. The simplest arrangement is to have an entrance into the shelter, as you will need to feed the birds here every day. You can enter the flight via the shelter as you will need to go into this part of the aviary only every week or two, to clean the floor. Try to arrange the doors so they are as unobtrusive as possible.

The shelter needs to be dry and well lit, to encourage the birds to roost here at night, so they will be protected from predators, such as foxes and cats, and bad weather.

Tongued-and-grooved timber or heavy-duty marine plywood on a wooden frame are popular materials for the shelter. Set a window in one side, to provide natural light, and cover it with aviary mesh on its inner face, to prevent the birds injuring themselves on the glass. If you decide to construct a block of aviaries, then you will need to position windows at the back of each shelter unit.

It is a good idea to incorporate a safety porch into the design of the aviary. This is usually sited around the external door of the shelter, but you may also decide to place one at the end of the flight if you have an entrance point here. The porch, which you can construct of flight panels, will prevent any birds escaping when you enter the aviary. The arrangement of the doors is important here; hang the outer door of the porch so that it opens outwards and the one into the shelter to open inwards. This will give you enough room to enter the aviary with cleaning tools or perches when necessary. Fix a bolt on the inside of the safety porch door, to ensure it remains firmly closed while you are inside.

If you choose to build a small block of flights, then you can incorporate a service corridor, with a single entry point at one end. You may be able to do away with the safety porch with such an arrangement, since the birds will be secure in the shelters, which have their own doors linking them to the corridor. Again, fit bolts on these doors to ensure that they remain closed when not in use. The extra space within the corridor will give you room for storage.

Most shelters have a sloping roof, the highest aspect adjoining the flight. You will need to fix guttering along the lower edge to drain away rainwater, and so prevent you being soaked by the run-off as you move in and out of the safety porch.

To ensure that the interior of the shelter stays dry, cover the roof with a double layer of heavy duty roofing felt. (You can check for, and fill, any gaps here once you have assembled the structure.) Ensure that the felt overlaps the edges of the roof and that it is firmly battened in place around the edges, otherwise it is likely to be torn off in a gale. You can help to prolong the lifespan of the felt by painting it white. This reflects the sun's heat and so prevents the felt splitting prematurely. Replacing the felt, and carrying out any other repair work on the aviary, will cause considerable disturbance to the birds and will necessitate removing them from the aviary. This is not really feasible if the birds are breeding, as it may well cause them to desert their nest. It therefore pays to buy the best available material, rather than using a cheap grade with a limited lifespan.

Provide access to and from the shelter for the birds by cutting an entrance hole near the top of the shelter, next to (rather than as part of) the door. The size and height of the hole will depend on the species concerned, but 30cm(1ft) square is adequate even for macaws. Fix a landing platform, made from timber or thick plywood, beneath the entrance hole on either side. The depth of the platform will depend on the size of the bird, but, again, 30cm(1ft) on either side will be sufficient. Brackets provide the simplest means of supporting the platform. You may want to add

Reinforcing the frames

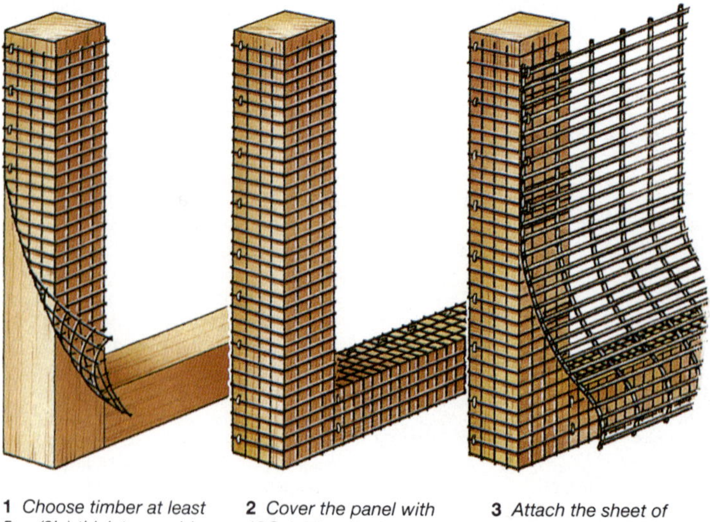

1 *Choose timber at least 5cm(2in) thick to provide a greater surface area on which to attach the mesh using netting staples.*

2 *Cover the panel with 19G 1.25cm(0.5in) square mesh to protect the woodwork from the parrots' powerful beaks.*

3 *Attach the sheet of mesh (size 2.5x1.25cm/ 1x0.5in or smaller) to the frame, tucking exposed ends underneath.*

Reinforcing the entrance hole

Above: *Use tin sheeting to protect woodwork surrounding the entrance hole from the strong beaks of some species. Fold back any sharp pieces of metal, so that the birds cannot cut their feet.*

vertical edges, creating an open box structure, to protect the interior of the shelter from direct winds. This is especially important with Grey Parrots, which, even when acclimatized, dislike cold weather.

Erecting the aviary

It is important to prepare the site properly for the aviary. Start by clearing the area, and cutting away any turf. Try to position the aviary so that the proposed entrance will be near a path. Store the turf in a cool, shaded spot in the garden for replanting once you have finished the work. Some damage to an existing lawn will be inevitable and it is also advisable to cut back any tall shrubs or trees that overhang the site. Protruding branches are certain to be damaged as you lift the panels into position and, once the aviary is finished, they will provide perches for wild birds, whose droppings may spread disease to the aviary birds.

Prepare secure foundations for the structure by digging a trench around the perimeter and setting blocks to a depth of about 30cm(1ft), and a similar height above ground. These will anchor the aviary firmly in place and will also make it difficult for vermin to burrow into the flight, even if you do not have a solid concrete base.

A concrete floor will add to the cost of the aviary and will be a fairly permanent fixture, but it will be easy to keep clean and is a precaution against rodents, so lessening the risk of disease. The concrete should be laid on a well-compacted bed of hardcore, the final covering being sloped to a drainage hole at the far end of the flight so that water drains away. (You may decide to call in a plasterer to achieve the correct finish.) If the mix is too sandy, the surface will start to break up, and algal growth will appear in the gaps, which will spoil the appearance of the aviary.

As an alternative, you may decide to opt for paving slabs. However, it is hard to establish a proper gradient with these and you may find that flooding is a problem during periods of heavy rainfall.

Drainage can also be a problem with a gravel floor, unless you lay the stones at least 25cm(10in) deep. Place a sheet of wire mesh over the floor between the bed of hardcore and the gravel layer to act as a barrier against rodents.

Grass may seem the obvious choice for the floor of the flight, but is far from ideal in practice, unless the aviary is very large. Water-logging can be a major problem, particularly in small areas, causing moss, and even fungi, to thrive. It is also difficult to clear up the birds' droppings, although slabs set into the grass beneath perches will facilitate this task.

Perches in the aviary

A good supply of perches will serve to distract the parrots from any woodwork in the aviary. As in an indoor flight, these should be positioned across the aviary, rather than lengthways. It is important to leave adequate flying space within the flight; in most cases, two main perches located at each end of the flight will be sufficient. Avoid positioning perches too close to the ends of the aviary, or parrots may damage their tails.

Fix the perches in place by twisting wire around the vertical supports of the framework, fixing it in place with netting staples. Try not to force the branches against the mesh or, over a period of time, you will weaken the aviary structure in the process.

You can also set branches in large pots or tubs, to create a tree-like effect. (There is no point attempting to plant trees or shrubs in the aviary, as even parrotlets will destroy any vegetation.)

Aviaries for other parrots

Accommodation for larger parrots will need to be reinforced to withstand the onslaught of their more powerful beaks. Choose 5cm(2in) timber for the flight panels, to provide a greater surface area on which to attach the mesh (again, using netting staples). The mesh size should not exceed 2.5x1.25cm(1x0.5in), not only to exclude rodents, but also to prevent the parrots reaching through it to gnaw on the timber.

It is particularly important with the larger species that you fully cover the inner surfaces of the flight panels with mesh, so that they are not accessible to the parrots' beaks. As an additional precaution, tack a layer of 19G 1.25cm(0.5in) square mesh around the inner surface of the frame before applying the thicker mesh on top to cover the panel.

You will also need to protect the shelter by lining the interior with mesh so that none of the framework supports are exposed to the birds. Parrots will not be able to chew a flat surface, but if they find

Below: *A brick structure is ideal for the larger, more destructive parrot species. This one houses a pair of rare Red-fronted Macaws.*

Above: *An all-metal suspended aviary in an indoor breeding unit. Note the position of the nestbox, allowing inspection from outside.*

any unprotected edges, they will destroy the timber easily.

A major area of weakness is likely to be the landing platform. You can protect the woodwork here by folding tin sheeting tightly over the exposed edges. Check that the metal is flat against the surface of the shelter and extend it about 10cm(4in) down the sides to minimize the risk of the parrots cutting their toes on the sharp edges of the metal. You may be able to bend the bottom cut edges up behind the sheeting so that they are completely out of reach.

As a result of the problems involved in constructing a durable aviary for the larger parrots, several companies have now started to market all-metal structures, complete with shelter. These are ideal in many respects, although some shelters lack windows. Although at first glance a metal aviary may appear quite expensive, it will save you the considerable time and trouble necessary to parrot-proof a more conventional wooden aviary. Although you can keep *Poicephalus* species, Grey Parrots, vasas, and even pionus quite satisfactorily in the home-built surroundings previously described, a metal structure undoubtedly provides a better option for the large macaws. As with timber-framed aviaries, sectional designs are preferable, so that you can build the aviary to meet your own requirements.

Some parrot-keepers build shelters out of bricks or concrete blocks. These aviaries, too, should be fairly indestructible, but don't forget to include damp-proofing. Remember, also, that you are more likely to need planning permission for a building of this type, as it may be considered more permanent than a traditional wooden aviary.

Suspended flights

As the cost of materials needed to build an aviary has risen, so birdkeepers have sought cheaper and more efficient designs of aviary. Suspended flights – all-wire cages supported off the ground on block or brick pillars – have become popular, particularly in North America.

Although, in theory, suspended flights may appear an ideal option, in reality, they are difficult to service. A simple task, such as replacing perches, becomes a problem, while the droppings are as likely to stick on the mesh as to accumulate on the floor. (The mesh needs to be at least 2.5cm/1in square over the floor area for this reason.) Whereas a conventional flight can be anchored all around using framefixers driven through to the framework, the suspended flight can be fixed only to the brick supports and is thus less secure.

Raised shelters can also be useful in some situations. Here, of course, you will need a safety porch not only around the shelter door, but also around any entrance to the flight. Do not rely on entry to the shelter only through the flight, because this will disturb the birds when they are breeding here. Amazons, especially, may become aggressive during the breeding period, and might attack you when you pass close to their nestbox.

Above: *Although they are cost efficient, raised aviaries, such as these, are not ideal, because of the problem of access to the interior.*

The birdroom

Suspended flights can be valuable in the birdroom, where you will not have to worry so much about secure access points. You can position opening flaps within reach of perches, to give you access to food pots, and attach a nestbox to the outside of the flight, at one end. A number of such flights can be installed in a birdroom, and by placing sheets of newspaper beneath, it is a straightforward matter to keep the floor clean.

If a number of parrots are being kept in an enclosed space, the atmosphere can become quite dusty, especially during the moulting period. The dust develops from the sheaths in which the developing feathers emerge through the skin, and is broken down, often by preening. Dust can cause an allergy, especially if you suffer from asthma, and so you should try to eliminate it from the environment as far as possible.

Regularly spraying all parrots kept indoors (either in a birdroom or in the home), not only helps to maintain the condition of the parrot's plumage, but will also dampen the dust particles. Direct the spray above the parrot's head, taking care to avoid the seed pots, so that the droplets fall on the bird like rain. The fine mist produced by plant sprayers is ideal for this purpose. Use tepid rather than cold water, and avoid spraying the parrots during particularly cold weather, to prevent them developing a chill. Although they may be nervous at first, most parrots soon actively look forward to having a shower, calling loudly when they see the sprayer.

Another means of combating dust in a birdroom is to use an ionizer. This device requires an electrical supply, but some models will operate off car batteries. The ionizer operates by producing a stream of high-energy electrons from the tip that combine with dust particles in the atmosphere, imparting a negative charge to them. This causes them to be precipitated to an earthed surface, leaving the air clean. You will then need to mop the floors of the birdroom with a damp cloth.

A recent innovation has been the development of electronic air cleaners. Whereas an ionizer will precipitate dust, and destroy a large percentage of harmful and other micro-organisms in the air, a cleaner of this type actually purifies the air by removing the pollutants directly. At present, however, cleaners of this type are both more expensive to buy and more costly to operate than ionizers.

Security

Unfortunately, as the price of parrots has risen, so has the number of thefts. It is virtually impossible to track down stolen birds, unless they are identifiable. Rings may be useful for your own identification purposes, but a thief can remove them quite easily before selling the birds, often to an unsuspecting purchaser. Tattoos are not very useful, either, as they eventually become obscured.

An increasing number of birdkeepers, particularly in North America at present, are now turning to microchip implants as a means of reliable identification to protect against thefts. The veterinarian anaesthetizes the bird and implants a tiny microchip, contained in a glass capsule, into the muscle of the breast. This microchip contains a unique code, which is read by a special scanner. Testing has confirmed that this is a very safe and reliable method of marking, and thus identifying, large, valuable parrots, in particular. For further details, ask a veterinarian who is familiar with psittacines.

Below: *A service corridor for a block of aviaries. Access for feeding and cleaning is simple and a solid partition separates the pairs.*

Apart from marking the birds themselves, there are a number of general security precautions you can take. Parrots and macaws housed in outside aviaries are most at risk from thieves; firstly, because their calls are likely to attract attention, and, secondly, because gaining access to an aviary is relatively straightforward compared with breaking into a birdroom or even your home.

For professional advice on protecting your collection, contact your local police office; they may well have a crime prevention specialist who can help you. There are also private security firms who may offer their own systems. Possible options include pressure pads, disguised in the safety porch, for example, and infrared beams connected to powerful floodlights and an alarm in your house.

Try to position the aviary so that it will be as inconspicuous as possible from the road, and don't forget the basic precaution of locking it, which will at least deter casual vandals. An alert dog can also be a valuable asset to deter potential burglars, while taking care over visitors, especially if you are selling birds, is also recommended. This need not be obvious; simply logging their car number-plates could prove a useful starting point for any police investigation should you be unfortunate enough to suffer a theft.

Several insurance companies now offer policies that protect clients against their birds being stolen, and it may be worth you considering one of these if your collection is large enough. Premiums are generally lower for parrots housed indoors (in your home or in a birdroom) and further discounts may be negotiable on the basis of the security measures you have in force. Do check the small print of a policy, however, noting any restrictions or exclusions carefully.

Feeding parrots and macaws

Advances in nutritional knowledge are among the main factors that have led to repeated breeding successes with these birds in recent years. Complete diets, containing all the ingredients believed necessary to keep parrots in good health and encourage breeding, are widely available today and a number have now been used for years with excellent results.

Complete diets

The main problem with using this type of diet is that it can be difficult to persuade parrots to sample such food, in spite of the fact that complete diets offer a much more balanced alternative to a traditional parrot seed mixture, comprised mainly of sunflower seed and peanuts. However, now that more parrot chicks are being raised by hand, it is becoming easier to persuade them to eat a complete diet. A number of the hand-rearing formulae on offer also have an equivalent weaning diet, which means that young parrots can be transferred onto this food very easily, especially as they are already used to the taste.

In the case of adult birds confronted with this unfamiliar foodstuff, it may be worth adding the complete diet to their regular seed mix in the hope that their curiosity will encourage them to sample it. This method can be particularly useful with macaws, which, instead of taking seeds singly from the food pot will scoop up a number at once. They then store the seeds under their prehensile tongue, and crack and swallow the kernels individually.

African parrots such as the Senegal can prove difficult to transfer to a complete diet, but once one member of a pair is feeding readily on this food, then its partner is likely to follow this example. Once the birds reach this stage, you can begin to gradually increase the amount of the complete food in the mix.

Factors such as shape may have an impact in determining the parrot's level of interest. Fairly short,

Below: *Nuts provide a welcome treat for most parrots. This Blue and Gold Macaw is enjoying a brazil, which it has cracked with its beak.*

thick nuggets, which resemble seeds, are usually preferable to long, thin pellets. Colour appears to be less significant, although many ranges contain bright, 'natural' colours. It is important to check that the size of the diet is suitable for the species concerned.

You may also find that some brands are available in two forms: a maintenance diet suitable for non-breeding stock including pet parrots, plus a breeding diet, which contains a higher level of protein.

Make the change between these diets over a period of two weeks, about a month before the likely start of the breeding period. The breeder ration should have a stimulating effect on the parrots, and will also be of value to the adult birds once they are rearing chicks.

Seeds and nuts

In spite of the nutritional benefits of a complete diet, it is not always possible to switch adult birds to this type of food easily. In addition, if they become bored, pet parrots, especially, may resort to crushing up this type of food aimlessly rather than eating the nuggets. If this happens, you may need to offer a mixed diet that includes a range of seeds and nuts for extra variety. Most parrot mixtures are based on sunflower, with other seeds such as hemp added in small amounts. Hemp can be recognized by its brownish colour and circular shape.

Striped sunflower seed is more commonly available than the white form, but the latter is nutritionally superior, with a slightly higher level of protein and a lower oil (fat) content. Avoid purchasing large grades of sunflower seed, as the inner kernel, which is the only part of the seed that is eaten, tends to be of a fairly standard size, irrespective of the grade. The smaller seeds are better value, because there is less wastage.

Another oil seed, safflower, is easily confused with white sunflower but has a more rotund shape. Valued for its protein content, safflower is especially popular with the medium-sized parrots, such as the *Poicephalus* species, but their favourite items in a seed mix are groundnuts, or loose peanuts. Again, it is wasteful to purchase unshelled nuts to add to a seed mix, because the husk will be discarded. Purchase your seed only from reputable suppliers, because peanuts, for example, can be the source of the deadly fungal poisons called aflatoxins. These will develop if the seed is stored under damp conditions, and can cause irreversible damage to the liver.

Nuts are often appreciated by the larger parrots, in particular, and a variety may be available on a seasonal basis. Pine nuts are usually available throughout the year and even parrotlets can crack the small Chinese variety without too much difficulty, while the large grades are suitable for the other species covered in this book. Check supplies carefully for any signs of green mould; you are most likely to discover this on damaged nuts where the kernel is exposed.

Some pet stores stock pine nuts, but you may need to go to a supermarket or health food store for other nuts. Brazil nuts have a tough outer casing, but this can be cracked quite easily by the larger macaws. Walnuts are another favourite, and hazelnuts, too, are likely to be greedily consumed by parrots as an addition to their usual seed mixture. If you crack the nuts yourself, you can offer pieces to your bird and allow it to extract the kernel. Never buy salted nuts of any kind to feed to birds, as the salt can prove harmful to them.

Parrot mixes

Branded parrot foods probably offer the best guarantee of quality and cleanliness, being produced to a high standard, but are, consequently, a rather expensive alternative to buying seed and mixing it yourself. Good mixes will include pumpkin seeds, which are broad, flat and whitish in colour, and red chilli peppers, often favoured by amazons and macaws, in addition to the above-mentioned seeds and nuts. (Only the larger parrots will be able to crush the whole grains, which are likely to be discarded by other species.)

Some parrot food mixtures also contain a variety of dried fruits and vegetables, such as carrot, apricot, pineapple, banana, and even alfalfa cubes (a form of grass), which are popular with many parrots. (It is worth noting that the nutritional value, in terms of carbohydrate, of dried fruit tends to be several times higher than that of fresh fruit.)

Feeding parrotlets

Parrotlets have rather different dietary requirements from those of the larger parrots. Their basic seed mixture should be comprised of millets and plain canary seed, as offered to budgerigars. Parrotlets are often keen on millet sprays, which, like other seeds, such as sunflower, can be soaked rather than fed dry. This improves their nutritional value, especially in terms of protein, while the softened, germinating seed is more digestible. (It is for these reasons that soaked seed is often supplied as a rearing food.)

Prepare the millet spray by immersing it in warm water and leaving it to stand for about 24 hours before rinsing it thoroughly under a running tap. Remember that soaked seed is a perishable foodstuff and you must discard any surplus within a day, as it can rapidly turn mouldy, especially in warm weather.

Choosing and storing foodstuffs

Seed that has been properly cleaned should not be dusty. If it does appear dirty, there is a risk that debris, such as stones, or even sharp pieces of glass, could be present along with seed. Check that it smells fresh; a sickly sweet odour is usually indicative of fodder mites. These feed on the seed, rather than attacking the birds, but may spread disease through contamination. As it is not possible to eliminate fodder mites from seed effectively and safely, you will have to discard the affected seed.

Rodent droppings are another obvious menace to the parrots' health, and contaminated seed will almost certainly have been exposed to their urine as well. Obviously, you will have to dispose of it. To prevent rodents gaining access to seed, always store it out of their reach in metal bins.

Keep a sharp watch for any sign of rodent activity in the aviary. The sudden appearance of a mound of earth suggests the presence of rats, whereas mice are more likely to be betrayed by their droppings, particularly near the parrots' food pots. It is vital to eliminate rodents quickly; at the very least, they will disturb the birds, and rats may even kill parrots. There is also a constant disease risk, both to the birds and to you, from rodents, and they can prove very destructive within an aviary.

Good hygiene in the aviary is vital; without a reliable food source, rodents will not be attracted to the area. Feed the birds in the shelter and clean up thoroughly once or twice a week, so that spilt seed is not left to accumulate on the floor. If you suspect that mice could be entering the aviary, remove the seed pots just before dusk, sweep up any spilt seed, and only replace the pots the next morning. This should not cause the parrots any distress, but should dissuade mice, which normally feed after dark, from becoming established here.

Unfortunately, some seed and husks are bound to fall down between the mesh and the timber-clad wall of the shelter. Leave the netting staples protruding slightly near the floor so that you can pull them out easily to sweep behind the mesh. If you line the floor of the shelter with clean newspaper, you will be able to tidy up spilt seed and other foods without difficulty, discarding the soiled sheets.

Because of the greater numbers of birds and more loose seed in the birdroom, the problem of rodent activity can be worse here, particularly if the structure is lined with insulating material. Eliminating mice that are nesting behind this

Feeding parrots and macaws

Species	**Seed**	**Fruit and greenstuff**
Parrotlets	Canary seed, millet (seed and sprays) plus some groats and sunflower. A parakeet mix is ideal.	Chickweed, seeding grasses and sweet apple.
Amazons, pionus and vasa parrots	Pine nuts, sunflower seed, groats, peanuts, safflower and millet sprays.	Fruit and vegetables; not avocados, as these may prove poisonous.
Macaws	As above. Smaller species may take millet and canary seed. Larger macaws enjoy brazils and whole maize.	Prefer fruit, but also eat carrot and some greenfood.
Grey Parrot, *Poicephalus* parrots	A good parrot mix, plus a limited amount of peanuts.	Prefer fruit to greenfood. Often reluctant to try unfamiliar items.
Eclectus and Great-billed Parrots	Parrot seed mix.	Plenty of greenfood (limit cabbage; it has a depressive effect on the thyroid glands). Also corn-on-the-cob, carrot and a variety of fruit.

lining can prove a costly and unpleasant task. You may want to incorporate an ultrasonic rodent scarer as a deterrent. This device emits high frequency sounds, which are inaudible to the human ear and cause no adverse reactions in parrots, but which are highly disorientating to rodents.

Although you can use more traditional means of eradication in the aviary, poisons and most killer traps are potentially very dangerous to birds as well as mice. You will need to rely on safe traps that will catch the rodents alive. Most of the designs that are advertised in the birdkeeping magazines work on the same principle. The mice are attracted into the empty base of the unit by seed. After a few nights, you set the lid in place, and the mice, while still able to enter the trap, find themselves unable to escape. Such traps provide an efficient means of dealing with a large number of mice, as they can catch a dozen or more at a single setting.

Fresh food

As well as a combination of dry seeds and pellets, parrots also require a regular supply of fresh fruit and greenstuff. The choice available will obviously depend to some extent on where you live, and usually varies seasonally. In temperate regions, apples and grapes are traditionally popular foods for parrots, but there is no reason why you cannot feed other more exotic fruits, such as mango, to provide variety. You should always wash perishable items of this nature thoroughly before offering them to the parrots.

Macaws can hold a whole apple without difficulty, and appear to enjoy gnawing chunks out of it, but you may need to cut fruit into pieces for smaller parrots. Cutting up the fruit also prevents wastage – parrots may throw a whole apple, or other fruit, on the floor, rather than eat it. Cut fruit provides an ideal means of adding a food supplement to the parrot's diet; the dry supplement will stick to its wet

surface, whereas it often just accumulates at the bottom of a seed pot.

Although the African species generally prefer fruit, greenstuff is also popular with a number of parrots. The choice of greenstuff depends to some extent on the species; parrotlets, for example, favour chickweed (*Stellaria media*) and seeding grasses, whereas macaws and amazons prefer the thick succulent stems of perpetual spinach. This is a crop that can be grown easily in the garden from seed and will even survive throughout the winter.

Should you have a parrot that refuses fresh food, try offering some greenfood on top of the seed. Avoid feeding frozen greenfood, as it could cause a digestive upset, and remember to wash fruit and greenstuff in case it has been contaminated by wild birds. Parrots may well discard the leaves of spinach beet, eating just the stalks. You must remove these and other uneaten food at the end of the day.

Food and drink containers

Seed pots sold for budgerigars will be suitably robust for parrotlets. Position these open containers close to perches in the shelter, fixing them onto the mesh. Avoid filling them right to the top, to prevent seed being scattered around the floor. Hold millet sprays in place with a metal clip (or a wooden clothes peg for parrotlets).

Above: *Solid, heavyweight feeding bowls are ideal for parrots. Make sure that you wash every day any that have been used for fresh food.*

For larger parrots, you may be able to purchase stainless steel feeding containers, which bolt onto the mesh. The bowl section will detach from the arm for ease of cleaning. Loose stainless steel bowls are less satisfactory, as they are light and thus easily overturned.

The best option for large macaws is a heavy ceramic bowl, as sold in pet stores for dogs. You can fill this either with seed or fresh items, and place it on top of the newspaper lining the shelter. The parrots will be unable to overturn such a large, heavy bowl, and it will be easy to clean when it becomes soiled. (Wash out bowls used for fresh foods every day.)

Parrots feeding on a complete diet drink more water than those on a diet of seed, but fresh, clean drinking water should always be available to all parrots. You can provide an uncontaminated supply in a special drinking bottle with a stainless steel spout, which fits through the mesh of the birds' quarters and which you can easily replenish from outside, without having to disturb the parrots. Place the drinker above a perch at a convenient height for the parrot.

It can be difficult to fix a drinking bottle securely within the shelter of an aviary. If you have to hang it on the outside of the flight, choose a sheltered location, as direct sunlight will trigger greenish algal growth on the sides of the bottle, while the water in the spout is likely to freeze in cold weather. Avoid filling the drinker to its maximum capacity in cold weather or it may split as the water expands on freezing.

If you administer a tonic in the drinking water, you should wash out the drinker thoroughly on the following day, using a special bottle brush, and if you use a detergent or disinfectant to clean it, be sure to rinse the bottle and spout thoroughly before re-using them.

Ceramic bowls are not really suitable for drinking water as they are easily polluted with food and droppings. With some birds, however, you may have no other choice; large macaws, especially, may play with the spouts of bottle drinkers, crushing the stainless steel tubes in their beaks.

Grit, minerals and supplements

Parrots do not have teeth of any kind but rely instead on a muscular organ called the gizzard to break up the food particles. Seed moves from the crop, at the base of the neck, via the proventriculus (a glandular area of the digestive tract) to the gizzard.

Grit helps to grind down the seed kernels and other food in the gizzard, as it is rubbed abrasively against the food particles by the muscular walls of this organ. In time, the grit itself will be broken down, releasing its mineral content, which will then be absorbed into the parrot's body.

While parrotlets will take budgerigar grit, larger parrots often seem reluctant to consume grit of any size, and whether or not to supply grit for larger parrots has long been a source of dispute among birdkeepers. Nevertheless, for the larger species, pigeon grit (as sold for racing pigeons) is recommended. Top up the grit container regularly, so that the parrots can forage for particles of their choice. In some cases, parrots will swallow wood chips, gnawed from perches, and these perform a similar function to grit when they reach the gizzard.

You should also offer the parrots calcium, in the form of cuttlefish bone, or a block. This mineral is very important for healthy bone structure, and a lack of it, particularly when the birds are young, can result in permanent skeletal weaknesses. Calcium is also particularly vital for breeding hens. Soft-shelled eggs can arise as a result of a deficiency, especially in the more free-breeding species, such as the Eclectus Parrot, and further complications, notably egg-binding, may develop as a result. Gnawing on a cuttlefish bone will also help to keep the parrots' beaks from becoming overgrown.

Vitamin and mineral supplements are important for parrots being kept mainly on a diet of seed. They should not be used regularly with birds being fed on a complete diet, because this already contains all the essential ingredients in the correct proportions. Using a supplement will result in vitamin overdosing, which is likely to be harmful over a period of time. To ensure the maximum value of a complete diet, check the expiry date on the pack, and do not purchase a large quantity at once. This type of food must be kept dry like seed and should ideally be stored in air-tight conditions.

Below: *A clever device for feeding parrots from the service corridor, this 'serving hatch' would be very useful for breeding pairs.*

Basic health care

Once established in their quarters, parrots are normally very healthy and long-lived. You will need to take care with recently imported birds, however, especially if you intend to keep them in an outdoor aviary. Although they will have been through a period of quarantine, such birds will not necessarily be acclimatized. A sudden drop in temperature, coupled with a change in environment, can easily trigger an illness that could prove fatal for your bird.

Try to minimize changes to your new parrot's environment by asking its seller about its diet and the temperature in which it has been kept. Even if the weather is mild, do not transfer a new bird straight into a flight with another parrot. The newcomer may be persecuted by the established bird (whether or not the two are of the same sex). Keep it in isolation for at least two weeks, or it could spread an infection to other birds.

General care of sick parrots

The signs of illness in parrots are fairly non specific in most cases, and accurate diagnosis is very difficult without tests. Unfortunately, such tests are generally impractical because, especially with bacterial and viral diseases, the bird's condition deteriorates rapidly and it may be too late to start an effective course of treatment if you wait for a diagnosis. As a result, broad-spectrum antibiotics, which are effective against a range of bacteria, are often prescribed at an early stage of an illness.

It is important that you check your parrots at least twice daily, to ensure that they are well. If you regularly spend a few moments looking at the birds, watching their general demeanour and how they move, you will be able to recognize when one falls ill. A sick bird will appear slightly dull and less active than usual. Its droppings also may have altered in appearance; instead of being well formed, they may turn watery, with a higher proportion of white uric acid (the urinary component) present. A parrot whose plumage appears ruffled, and that is sitting with both feet gripping the perch, and its eyes closed, showing little interest in its surroundings, is in need of urgent veterinary attention.

Below: *This Jardine's Parrot is clearly poorly. Sick parrots need rapid treatment; your veterinarian will often prescribe antibiotics at the first sign of ill health.*

Above: *Suspend a special infrared lamp over the cage of a sick bird to keep it warm. This helps the antibiotic treatment to take effect and thus aids the bird's recovery.*

When you catch the bird, you may also notice that, because the muscles of the breast have wasted, the breastbone is more prominent. This emaciated condition is sometimes referred to as 'going light'. Hopefully, the parrot will recover and this weight loss will then be made up.

For treating sick birds at home, you should invest in a dull-emitter infrared system. This will consist of a bulb that gives off heat rather than light, so that the bird will be kept warm and will not be dazzled or disturbed by bright light, plus a holder and a surrounding reflector shield, which helps to concentrate the infrared rays. Some systems also incorporate a control unit, enabling you to adjust the heat.

Suspend the lamp over the wire top of the bird's cage to create a thermal gradient here. The warmest position will be directly beneath the infrared bulb, while the temperature will fall slightly on either side, so that the bird can adjust its position according to its need for warmth.

Although you may be able to obtain a purpose-built hospital cage, these are less flexible than using an infrared lamp. The bird will be kept in poorly ventilated surroundings and, as it will not have room to move around, the temperature is likely to be either too hot or cold. Such cages are generally too small for parrots, although some designs may be suitable for parrotlets.

Parrots usually recover quite rapidly, provided that appropriate treatment is begun at an early stage. Once the bird begins to become more alert, lower the heat supply gradually to reacclimatize the bird. (A variable heat controller will be useful at this stage.) Be guided by the parrot's response; if it starts to appear uncomfortable, ruffling its plumage, then you will need to increase the temperature again. Avoid reducing the temperature too rapidly.

Bacterial diseases

A wide variety of bacteria can be linked with disease in parrots. A general course of antibiotic treatment will usually be prescribed by your veterinarian.

In its simplest form, antibiotic is available as a powder, to be mixed with the bird's drinking water. The solution generally needs to be made up twice daily to retain its potency. It is important to provide the antibiotic solution in glass or plastic containers, which will not react with the treatment.

The main problem with providing antibiotics in solution is that recovery is entirely dependent on the volume of fluid that the bird will drink. It may not consume enough for the drug to attain a therapeutic level within its body. (Don't be tempted to exceed the recommended dose of any medication, however, as this can lead to adverse side-effects.)

Your veterinarian may decide to administer the drug by a more direct means. It is relatively easy and safe to inject larger parrots with a suitable antibiotic preparation. Tablets may also be useful in certain circumstances, although the latter have to be placed directly inside the parrot's mouth – a hazardous undertaking with a large macaw! You will need another person to restrain the bird, while you place the tablet at the back of the bird's mouth on the tongue. Hold the beak closed for a few moments afterwards to ensure that the parrot swallows the tablet rather than spitting it out.

A third, though less commonly used, way of directly administering an antibiotic, is to pass a tube down into the crop, and flush antibiotic solution directly into this part of the digestive tract.

In all cases, it is important that you seek proper veterinary advice and that you follow the recommended treatment regimen. Birds usually show signs of rapid recovery once appropriate treatment has begun, and you should notice a distinct improvement within a day or so. With any course of antibiotics, you should complete the treatment, even if the bird appears to have recovered, or the bacteria may multiply again, attacking the already weakened parrot.

If the treatment proves unsuccessful, and the parrot dies, it is worth arranging an autopsy, especially if the bird was in contact with others in your collection. A post-mortem examination will identify the bacterium responsible for death, and it should then be possible to find a specific antibiotic for treatment of any other parrots that fall sick, thus enabling you to prevent further losses.

Enteritis A number of bacteria, such as *Escherichia coli*, can give rise to digestive problems, notably enteritis, before spreading into the blood stream and affecting the body organs. Good hygiene is vital to prevent the spread of enteric diseases; *E. coli* is often present in the environment, and can be spread via dirty hands, when you are cutting up fruit, for example. An affected parrot's droppings will alter in consistency, and, certainly in the later stages of infection, the bird's appetite will decline. If you suspect that a bird is suffering from such a disease, you can obtain confirmation of the cause by culturing the droppings, while administering an antibiotic.

Unfortunately, the beneficial bacteria normally present in the parrot's digestive tract are also likely to be adversely affected by a course of antibiotic treatment. This may interfere with the manufacture of certain B vitamins, for example, or even allow another harmful type of bacteria to gain easy access to the parrot's body.

In the past, some veterinarians have recommended natural live yoghourt, given on fruit, to help a parrot through this convalescent stage. Live yoghourt contains *Lactobacillus* bacteria, which will help to colonize and protect the gut. You may also be able to obtain *Lactobacillus* in a powdered form direct from your veterinarian, and administer it in a similar way.

A more recent innovation in this field has been the marketing of probiotic products to encourage the development of helpful bacteria after an illness. Such products, although not widely available at present, may be obtainable from more specialist pet shops and bird farms. They are usually sold with a pipette for accurate dosage, and can be administered on food, such as cut fruit or greenstuff.

Salmonellosis and Yersiniosis Try to establish how the infection gained access to the aviary. Two serious diseases, salmonellosis and yersiniosis, may well be introduced by rodents and are likely to result in heavy losses of birds. *Salmonella* bacteria often trigger bloodstained droppings, while yersiniosis can result either in sudden death, or a more prolonged illness, during which the parrot loses body condition and becomes progressively more depressed. Treatment is rarely successful, largely because of the damage caused to the liver by these bacteria. Yersiniosis can be diagnosed quite easily at a post-mortem examination, because it leads to white spots on the liver

Above: *After administering eye drops to a parrot, hold the bird for a few minutes to allow the medication to mix with its eye fluid. Gently restrain the bird in a towel.*

that are reminiscent of avian tuberculosis. For this reason it is also known as pseudotuberculosis.

Both these diseases can also be spread via rodents or infected birds to people, so take sensible precautions when handling a sick parrot. Wash your hands after touching the bird or its surroundings, keep it isolated, and clean its quarters thoroughly with a suitable disinfectant solution. Many disinfectants are less effective in dirty surroundings, so scrub the flight with water before washing it out with disinfectant. Don't forget to clean perches and foodpots, too, and rinse them off thoroughly if they are to be re-used.

Chlamydiosis The potentially most serious, though rare, disease affecting parrots is sometimes still described as psittacosis or ornithosis, although it is now more commonly called chlamydiosis. It is known to occur in a wide range of mammals, including sheep and cats, rather than just affecting birds. Its significance lies in the fact that it can be transmitted to people, producing severe influenza-like symptoms. Antibiotic treatment is usually effective, but on a very few occasions, the disease can be fatal.

Parrots entering quarantine are routinely medicated against chlamydiosis in various countries, but, unfortunately, reliable diagnosis of the infection can only be made in the laboratory. Your veterinarian will be able to carry out some preliminary tests, which, although they are not entirely reliable, may be helpful. The disease is spread when infective particles present in the droppings are inhaled. Body secretions, such as those from the nose and eyes, also represent a threat.

In spite of odd media scare stories, however, there is really no great likelihood of you or your family contracting chlamydiosis from keeping parrots, particularly if you acquire your stock from reputable dealers or breeders. It is perhaps worth remembering that there are only about 10 cases of people contracting the disease each year in the UK, and a high percentage of those affected have not even been in contact with birds. Unfortunately, smuggling of parrots, notably across the Mexican border into the United States, does occur, and these birds, which will not have been quarantined and received preventive medication, represent the greatest health hazard.

Swelling around the eyes This general symptom is sometimes linked with chlamydiosis, but may equally be noted with other more common diseases. Sometimes, of course, it will not be caused by a bacterial infection; a scratch may trigger an inflammation. You are most likely to encounter swelling of this nature in recently imported amazon parrots. A local infection can be implicated, causing a blockage of the nostril on the same side of the head, for example.

Your veterinarian will probably recommend the use of an ophthalmic ointment, which you will need to apply to the eyes three or four times daily to maintain an adequate concentration of the drug here, as the tear fluids will tend to wash it away.

Hold the parrot for a few moments after applying the ointment, or it is likely to smear the medication across the perch as soon as it is returned to its quarters. Alternatively, you can use drops, which will not stain the plumage surrounding the eye at all, but which can be more difficult to apply, especially if the parrot blinks at the critical moment.

Swelling can also be the result of a deficiency of Vitamin A in the diet. If you feed plenty of greenfood and other fresh items, such as carrot (which is rich in Vitamin A), along with a vitamin supplement, the bird's vision should soon return to normal. If the parrots have been receiving a balanced diet – which should include a nutritional supplement and plenty of greenfood – then the swelling is more likely to have an infective than a nutritional cause.

Fungal disease

Fungal diseases tend to be more common in recently imported birds, especially if they have received a poor diet. Antibiotics are not generally very effective against fungal diseases and, indeed, a prolonged course of treatment can actually trigger a secondary fungal infection in some cases.

Candidiasis This is a problem associated particularly with Indonesian parrots, such as the Eclectus and the Great-billed, which appear to need relatively high amounts of Vitamin A in their diet. This important vitamin is notably deficient in dry seed, and so birds receiving a seed-based diet are particularly vulnerable.

Symptoms of candidiasis are most likely to be apparent in the mouth. The affected parrot will play with its food, rather than eating it, and you may notice a sticky whitish discharge from the beak. If you look inside the mouth you will see whitish patches of the *Candida* fungus. You can obtain specific medication from your veterinarian, but you will also need to improve the bird's diet, to assist recovery and to prevent any recurrence.

Aspergillosis The other major fungal problem encountered in parrots is known as aspergillosis. Research is continuing into drugs to treat this disease and some promising remedies have been developed. This disease usually spreads through the bird's airways, from fungal spores that are inhaled. Difficulty in breathing follows, and the condition worsens as the fungus develops, especially if the bird is stressed. Aspergillosis is usually a chronic disease and an affected bird's health will decline over several months. Diagnosis can be confirmed by an endoscopic examination (see pages 50–1), when the strands of the fungus will be clearly visible. Treatment may be possible, provided that the condition is not too far advanced.

Viral diseases

Although generally uncommon in parrots, no effective treatments exist to counter viral diseases.

Newcastle disease The most serious viral disease affecting parrots is Newcastle disease, because it can be spread to poultry, and so results in a fall in egg-production. The possible effect of this disease is one of the major reasons why quarantine regulations are enforced for the movement of psittacines from one country to another. For further information on current quarantine regulations, you will need to contact your government department dealing with agricultural affairs. Provided that the parrots have been properly quarantined, there is little risk of them contracting this infection. Symptoms of infection vary, although neurological signs are often apparent.

Pacheco's disease Increasing concern has arisen during recent years over this disease, which is caused by a herpes virus. It is most commonly linked with parrots from Central and South America, although similar symptoms have been seen in African species. The disease usually becomes apparent during the quarantine period, although the susceptibility of individual genera appears to vary. In severe outbreaks, there can be very high mortality, especially among amazon parrots and macaws. Grey Parrots are also in the high risk category.

In many cases, there are few obvious signs, and large numbers of birds that have been eating and drinking normally have been known to die suddenly. Larger macaws may suffer a more protracted illness, often with a characteristic symptom of orange-coloured diarrhoea. The thirst of parrots suffering from Pacheco's disease will increase as a result of fluid loss you will need to guard against dehydration. Rarely will affected birds recover.

Research is continuing into the possibility of developing a vaccine to protect against Pacheco's disease. In the meantime, it is important to avoid adding recently imported conures, which are

Below: *Spraying parrots housed indoors with water helps prevent their plumage becoming too dry. You can also use an aerosol as a precaution against mites and lice.*

known to be symptomless carriers of the virus, to an existing collection of parrots. The problem seems to be more prevalent in species such as the Patagonian Conure (*Cyanoliseus patagonus*) and other parrots from the southern part of South America, than in those occurring further north.

Parasitic infestations

Although other members of the parrot family can suffer from a range of parasites, in most cases these do not represent a significant problem to the species covered in this book. As a precaution against various mites and lice, you will need to spray the birds with a suitable aerosol while they are in isolation with you. Be sure to use a product manufactured especially for use with birds (some of those marketed for dogs and cats may cause adverse reactions), and follow the instructions for use carefully.

Red mite is probably the most significant member of the group, largely because it will live in the parrots' surroundings, as well as feeding on the birds' blood. Thoroughly cleaning nestboxes at the end of each breeding season will help to prevent these parasites becoming established.

Various intestinal worms can be found in parrots, but these tend to be less common than in Australian parakeets. (However, if you keep parrotlets in accommodation previously used for these other species, they may become infected unless you thoroughly clean their quarters first.) The eggs of the roundworms are passed out in the birds' droppings, and represent a hazard to other individuals who may consume them. Good hygiene and appropriate medication will be essential to break the life-cycle of these parasites, which cause general ill health and, sometimes, weight loss in parrots.

It may be worth arranging for your veterinarian to screen the droppings of new birds. Should any evidence of these or other parasites be found, you can administer appropriate treatment during the isolation period, so preventing spread of the infection to established parrots.

Egg-binding

The reproductive problem you are most likely to encounter is egg-binding. This occurs when an egg forms a blockage in the lower part of a hen's reproductive tract, and she cannot expel it from her body. The underlying cause is usually in the surrounding muscles, which are responsible for forcing the egg out of the hen's body. Factors involved may include lack of muscle tone, cold weather (which decreases muscular activity) and low levels of calcium, (which is required for muscular contractions).

If keeping the affected hen in the warm for an hour or so proves fruitless, seek veterinary help immediately. The most effective treatment often proves to be an intramuscular injection of calcium gluconate, with a dose of 0.5mg per 100g of body weight. Although it may be possible to manipulate the egg out of the body, using a suitable lubricant, there is a risk that the egg could rupture, especially if it has a soft shell, leading to peritonitis (a severe infection of the body cavity).

In order to prevent egg-binding, be sure that the parrots have an adequate supply of cuttlefish bone, or a calcium block, throughout the year. The more prolific species, such as the parrotlets, should only be encouraged to breed during the warmer months of the year and restricted to a maximum of three clutches of eggs during this time.

Always keep a close watch on laying hens, so that you can spot the signs early, as this is a serious disorder that requires rapid treatment. An affected hen will usually emerge from the nestbox appearing unsteady on her feet. Before long, she will no longer be able to perch, and her legs may seem to be paralyzed. Once the egg is removed, the parrot should soon be able to perch normally, but you should not encourage her to breed again for a further year.

Preventing disease in the aviary

A number of potential dangers to your parrots' health lurk in and around the aviary. By taking precautions, you can prevent disease and ensure healthy stock.

New birds
Disease can be introduced to established stock by new arrivals. Keep them in quarantine for at least two weeks.

Perches
Avoid using dead wood for perches, as it may be contaminated with fungal spores. Parrots are susceptible to fungal diseases, including aspergillosis, which is difficult to treat.

Rusty mesh
Parrots use their beaks for climbing around their quarters, and rusty or badly galvanized wire in the aviary is therefore very dangerous. Sharp splinters may penetrate a bird's fleshy tongue or even embed in the wall of its crop.

Food pots
Dirty food containers provide a focus for bacterial and fungal growth. In particular, pots used for perishable foodstuffs, such as soaked seed, will need to be washed daily.

Plants
Certain plants and their seeds may be poisonous to birds. (In any case, parrots are likely to destroy any vegetation in their aviary.)

The aviary floor
A solid floor – concrete is ideal – will prevent rodents gaining access to the aviary and will be easy to keep clean.

Wild birds
Spilt seed will attract wild birds, which, if they can gain access to the flight, will not only steal the parrots' food, but may also spread disease and parasites. Ensure that the mesh is undamaged and that the dimensions of the strands are sufficiently small to exclude sparrows and other small birds.

Rodents
Rats and mice may enter the aviary via holes in the mesh, or by burrowing in through the floor. They will contaminate food, and may even harm the birds directly. Eliminate them without delay, using suitable live traps.

Breeding and rearing parrots and macaws

Provided that you have a compatible pair of parrots, there is no reason why they should not nest satisfactorily, even in indoor surroundings. Because of the long incubation and rearing periods of the larger parrots, they will normally lay only one clutch of chicks when housed in an outdoor aviary in most temperate areas. Eclectus Parrots tend to be an exception, however, as they will lay repeatedly, and parrotlets are also prolific, sometimes nesting several times during a breeding season.

In some years, you may find that an established pair do not attempt to breed. While a change in their environment may be responsible, it could be simply that they are resting. (The latest field research from Peru has revealed that the large macaws often only nest every second or third year in the wild.)

Sexing methods

In the past, one of the major problems associated with breeding most of the parrots and macaws featured in this book was that it was impossible to identify the sex of individual birds reliably by visual means. This meant that many supposed pairs were simply birds of the same sex housed together.

Mutual preening and feeding are not clear indicators of breeding pairs, since two birds kept together for any length of time may behave in this fashion, irrespective of their sex. In some cases, it may be possible to detect slight variances in physical appearance; hen macaws, for example, have a narrower head and are slightly smaller overall than their male counterparts. But such differences could be due equally to regional variations, bearing in mind that many of these species have a very wide distribution.

In recent years, there have been a number of significant advances in methods of sexing parrots that are not sexually dimorphic. Here we examine the four main methods which have been used: surgical sexing, karyotyping, DNA analysis and faecal steroid analysis.

Surgical sexing The advent of surgical or endoscopic sexing has overcome this problem, and can also provide valuable insight into the overall health and reproductive state of the individual parrot. The technique entails direct visualization of the bird's body cavity, using a narrow probe called an endoscope. A veterinarian will carry out this procedure for you, and will also be able to advise on the treatment of any problems, such as infection of the air-sacs, which he may notice at the same time (see panel opposite).

You will probably need to withhold food from parrots on the night before they are to be sexed, but you can check this with your veterinarian in advance. If you suspect that the bird may be poorly, particularly if it is suffering from a respiratory problem, you should inform the veterinarian, as, if nothing else, this may affect the choice of anaesthetic. Obese parrots also present possible complications, and if you have recently acquired a bird that has been kept as a pet for a long period, it may be wise to get it fit in aviary surroundings before taking it to your veterinarian to be sexed.

The veterinarian may give the bird a gaseous anaesthetic or use an injectable compound. Recovery is surprisingly quick after the former, but in either case, you should keep the parrots quiet in the post-operative period. The site of the tiny incision, on the left flank, heals rapidly and does not usually require stitching. Overall, surgical sexing is very safe, especially in experienced hands, and generally reliable, although it will not be possible to guarantee the sex of recently fledged young birds.

A number of dealers now offer surgically sexed pairs of parrots for sale. (The initials 'S.S.' alongside the pair in question will indicate that they have been sexed in this way.) They may also offer a veterinary certificate to this effect to intending purchasers, but this provides no absolute guarantee of sex, unless the parrots are either rung or

Surgically sexing a parrot

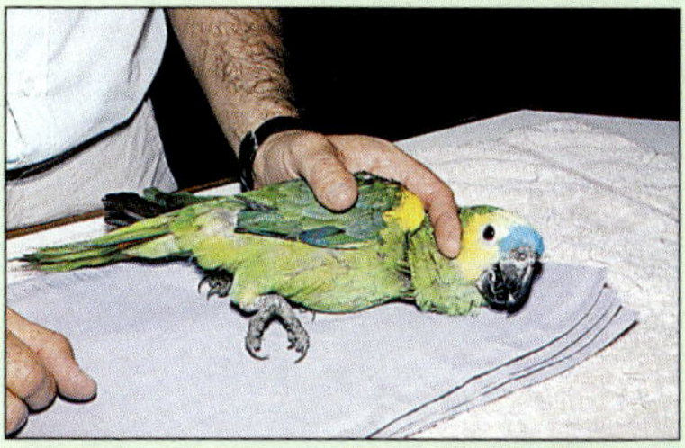

Stage One
The veterinarian will restrain the parrot and give it an anaesthetic. This bird has been injected, but some veterinarians will prefer to use a gaseous agent. You may need to withhold food from the parrot on the test day.

Stage Two
The site for the incision – on the left-hand side behind the last rib – is prepared by removing a few feathers and cleaning the area. This site is chosen because most hens retain only one functional ovary, located here.

Stage Three
The small hole into which the delicate endoscope will be inserted is being made here by an instrument known as a trocar. (This hole will not be sutured. By the time the bird has regained consciousness it will be barely visible.)

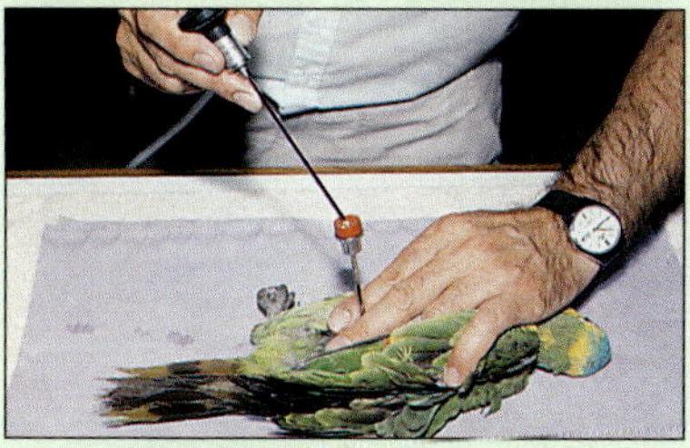

Stage Four
With the trocar in position, the delicate endoscope, with its black eye-piece, is carefully inserted into the body cavity. The inspection to determine the parrot's gender will take only a minute or two.

Stage Five
The endoscopic examination will not only enable the veterinarian to determine the sex of the parrot, but will also reveal any diseases, such as aspergillosis, which may be difficult to confirm by non-surgical means.

The standard parrot nestbox

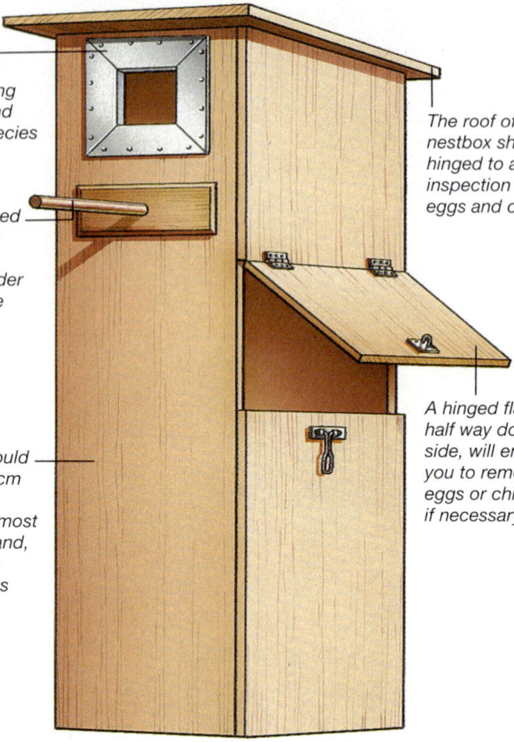

Above: *Note the metal sheeting used to reinforce the entrance to this nestbox, and the inspection flap, which must close securely. Incorporate an internal ladder.*

marked with a microchip implant (see page 35). Such details should be shown on the certificate. Although surgical sexing is reliable, there remains the slight possibility that a pair could have become mixed up after being sexed.

Laboratory techniques Faecal steroid analysis was the first of these methods to be used, seeking to sex birds on the basis of the relative differences in the levels of male and female sex hormones in their droppings. Unfortunately it was unreliable as it is dependant on a ratio in the first instance.

Chromosomal karyotyping then became very popular for a period in the mid-1980s. The karyotype is a map of the bird's chromosomes, present in the nucleus in every living cell in the body. The chromosomes, on which the genes are located, occur in pairs, with one specific pair being known as the sex chromosomes. They are responsible for determining the parrot's gender. In the hen, one member of this pair is shorter than the other chromosome.

Technically, this is quite a demanding procedure, and so with the growing advances in DNA technology, chromosomal karyotyping has now been superseded.

These laboratory methods have the advantages of being safer and more versatile than surgical sexing. There is no need to anaesthetize the parrot, as sufficient blood for analysis can be obtained from a

Other suitable nestboxes for parrots and macaws

Above and right: *Various other designs of nestboxes may be suitable for parrots. Converted beer casks, although difficult to inspect, are popular for the larger species, such as macaws. Adapted hollow logs may encourage reluctant pairs to nest, while for the smaller parrotlets you can provide the type of nestboxes used for budgerigars.*

plucked feather, dispatched to the laboratory in a special container, so the parrot does not even have to leave its quarters.

Another advantage with DNA sexing is that it can be carried out even before the chicks have left the nest. Obviously it is vital to be able to identify the individuals correctly or the results will be worthless.

Early sexing means that it is possible to decide immediately which birds you want to keep as part of an on-going breeding programme. This avoids pressure on accommodation, as you will not have to retain all the youngsters until they are sufficiently mature for surgical sexing to be reliable, which is likely to be well over a year in the case of the larger parrots.

One distinct advantage of surgical sexing is that it can assist in the detection of underlying illnesses such as the fungal ailment aspergillosis. Also, it can be used where a parrot is not breeding to determine whether there is any hidden disorder affecting the bird's reproductive system.

Nestboxes

Established proven pairs of parrots are likely to nest more readily in new surroundings than imported birds, which may well take three or four years to settle down before attempting to breed. Nevertheless, you should provide a nesting box from the outset, as many of the American parrots will prefer to roost here rather than on a perch.

If you do not want to construct your own nestboxes, you can purchase them, either in a kit form or ready assembled, from a pet store or specialist aviary manufacturer. The timber used needs to be at least 2.5cm(1in) thick in nestboxes intended for the larger parrots, and ideally double this thickness for macaws, which are the most destructive species.

The dimensions of the nestbox will obviously vary, depending on the species. Whereas parrotlets can be bred quite satisfactorily in budgerigar-type nestboxes, macaws will need a much larger structure. An internal area of about 25cm(10in) square will suffice for the *Poicephalus* species, while a slightly larger box should be adequate for pionus, Grey and amazon parrots. Allow a floor area of about 30cm(12in) square for the medium-sized macaws, and 45cm(18in) for the larger species.

The roof of the nestbox should be hinged, so that you can remove it for cleaning, and an inspection flap is also an advantage. This should be positioned on one of the sides, out of the parrots' reach when they are on the floor of the box, but located so that you can reach down inside if necessary. (An opening of this type will enable you to remove either eggs or chicks in an emergency, with the minimum of disturbance, and will also be useful if you intend to take the eggs away for artificial incubation.) You should attach a small bolt to the flap to ensure it remains securely closed when not in use.

The size of the entrance hole, which should be positioned near the roof of the box, will depend on the size of the parrots. If it is too small, then the birds will attempt to enlarge it. To calculate approximately the size the hole will need to be, measure across the broadest part of the parrot's back, at the top of its wings. As the more destructive species will persist in attacking this hole, it is worth protecting it by reinforcing it with tin sheeting (see page 31). You should ensure that there are no exposed edges, on which the parrots could cut their toes, by folding the sharp cut edges back out of their reach.

It is also usual to incorporate a simple ladder in the interior of the nestbox. By helping the parrots

Above: *This Green-winged Macaw is climbing out of its nestbox using an internal mesh ladder. This needs to be fixed securely in position, so that the parrots cannot dislodge it.*

climb in and out of the box, this ladder will minimize the risk of the birds accidentally harming their eggs or chicks. Aviary mesh, fixed in place with netting staples, is ideal for this purpose, but again, ensure that there are no sharp projections. Cutting a section off the side of a roll will give you one smooth edge, and you can then trim the opposite side, and the top and bottom of the ladder, to the nearest strand and file down the stubs until they are no longer sharp. Although you can simply tack this mesh on the inside of the box, from the entrance hole to the base, you may prefer to fix it first onto two lengths of thin battening, about 0.635cm(0.25in) thick, to create a miniature ladder. You can then attach this firmly in place in the nestbox using panel pins, driven through the battening onto the inner face below the entrance hole. If the parrots manage to dislodge the ladder, they will be unable to reach the eggs or chicks in the base of the box.

Although hollow logs often provide suitable nesting sites, they are not available to many birdkeepers. It can also be difficult to inspect the interior of the nesting chamber easily, and the parrots may eventually gnaw through the log, particularly if the wood is decaying. The interior may become contaminated with fungal spores, and will be harder to clean than a conventional nestbox.

Beer casks, usually made of oak, which is a fairly durable wood, and reinforced with metal supports, can be used successfully as a nesting site for macaws, instead of a more conventional box. Cut the entry point in the side, or at one end, and mount the cask on a sturdy base in the aviary. Because of its weight, you may need to provide support for such a nestbox in the form of a blockwork base. You should be able to attach smaller nestboxes to the aviary framework with brackets.

Position a conventional nestbox at a relatively high spot under cover in the aviary. Here there will be no risk of it being flooded during heavy rain, so chilling any eggs or chicks inside, and the parrots are less likely to be disturbed by cats or other animals. You may decide to offer a choice of nestboxes, positioning one in a fairly secluded spot outside in the flight, and the other in the shelter. Some parrots prefer fairly dark surroundings, and may ignore a nestbox in the flight. This seems to be especially true of *Poicephalus* parrots, which often nest more readily in the shelter.

Below: *These breeding cages house Yellow-faced Parrotlets. The nestboxes are placed at the back of the cages to give the birds a greater sense of security.*

Most nestboxes have a perch located just below the entrance hole, but as the parrots often destroy this at the start of the breeding period, it is worth positioning an aviary perch close to the entrance hole of the nestbox, so that the parrots can land here before darting into the nest.

The breeding period

In the wild, where they usually nest in tree holes, parrots and macaws will lay their eggs on a bed of wood chips. As the breeding period approaches, you will notice that the birds become far more destructive, attacking the perches and any exposed woodwork in their quarters with their beaks. In order to divert their attention, it is useful to provide blocks of softwood or lengths of battening on the floor of the nestbox. Both members of the pair will spend time in the nestbox, whittling down the wood to form a nest lining. This may be one of the earliest signs of breeding activity.

Carefully check the interior of the nestbox at regular intervals and add extra wood as it is whittled away. The wood chips will provide a clean and absorbent bed for the chicks when they hatch. Alternative nesting materials, such as peat, are likely to be scraped out of the box before the hen has laid, leaving the eggs at risk from chilling and damage, with nothing to stop them rolling around the box throughout the incubation period.

You may not see the parrots mating; they need to mate successfully only once in order to produce a fertile clutch of eggs. The hen will consume noticeably more cuttlefish bone during this period, and both members of the pair are likely to be more noisy than usual. As the time of laying approaches, the hen will spend increasing periods of time in the nestbox, although she may appear rather nervous at this stage, emerging at the slightest sound in the vicinity of the box. Even once she has laid her first white egg, she may continue to emerge regularly from the nestbox.

The incubation period

Most hens do not start incubating in earnest until they have laid a second or third egg. This helps to ensure that the chicks hatch closer together, so they will be of a more equal size, which favours their survival. All parrots lay white eggs, and those covered in this book usually lay on alternate days. The clutch size depends to some extent on the species.

You may detect a change in the behaviour of the parent birds as the breeding period progresses. This is particularly true of the larger parrots, notably macaws and amazons, which may become aggressive towards you, especially if you venture too near the nestbox. (It is for the same reason that tame birds kept as pets may undergo sudden character changes during the year, being more friendly at some times than others.) Try to avoid any conflict by leaving the parrots alone as much as possible. You can keep an eye on them from a distance to check that all is going well, and the food pots will provide an early indication of any problems. (If she is ailing for any reason, the hen, in particular, will consume less food than usual.)

Apart from an occasional case of egg-binding (see page 48), problems are rare through this stage, and incubation usually proceeds uneventfully. The hen sits alone, but may be joined for periods by her mate. She will usually emerge for a brief rest each day, often just after feeding time, or sometimes to take a bath in a shower of rain. Never be tempted to drive her out of the nestbox, or she may scatter, and possibly damage, her eggs.

Hatching problems

When calculating the incubation time, remember that this will be longer for the first, and possibly second, eggs, which will not have been incubated for the first few days. If the eggs fail to hatch, it may be simply that they were not fertilized, or that the embryo died at a very early stage, before it could develop. In either case, the eggs will appear translucent when held in front of a bright light.

Conversely, if an embryo formed, but failed to hatch, the eggs will be opaque. Such losses are often described as being 'dead in the shell'. There are far more potential causes in this case. It may be that the egg was damaged, and bacteria was thus able to penetrate the shell. Alternatively, insufficient fluid may have been lost through the shell pores during the incubation period, so that the chick failed to break through into its air space prior to hatching. Nutritional deficiencies and chilling are other factors that can lead to embryonic deaths. In such cases, it is possible that the parrots may lay again, even if they normally have only one clutch each breeding season.

The rearing period

There is no need to disturb the parent birds at the end of the incubation period. You will probably hear the young chicks begging for food before long, and only if they call persistently throughout the day is this a sign that something is amiss.

Parrots usually prove reliable parents, and once they have started breeding they will nest repeatedly over many years. But young, inexperienced pairs of macaws, for example, may lose their first chicks. It is difficult to know what to do for the best in such a situation; on the one hand, you will want to save the chicks, but on the other, the parent birds need to gain expertise. You can take the chicks away and raise them by hand if you feel that everything is not going well, but the problem may then simply recur the next time the birds breed.

The key with nervous birds is to avoid unnecessary interference. It may be possible to tempt the adult birds out at a regular time each day with their supplies of fruit and greenstuff. This will give you an opportunity to check the chicks quickly without causing a major disturbance to the nest.

Healthy chicks appear pinkish in colour, neither pale nor noticeably red. More significantly, a strong chick will normally raise its head to beg for food, especially if there is little remaining in its crop. This organ should be clearly visible at the base of the neck, its food contents appearing whitish through the skin. A chick should be reasonably capable of supporting itself, even at a young age, and one that lies on its side is definitely weak and sickly.

Artificially incubating and hand-rearing chicks

Hand-raising parrot chicks is a demanding occupation, especially as it will be several months before the offspring of the larger species can feed themselves. At first you will need to feed them about every two hours, virtually around the clock (although a longer gap from about 2 to 6 a.m. is acceptable), to ensure that they always have food in the crop. Although some birdkeepers allow a longer feeding interval, there is a risk that this will adversely affect the growth rate of the chicks over a period of time.

If you are not in a position to hand-raise chicks yourself, seek out the assistance of a professional to undertake this work for you for either a fee or a percentage of the chicks. You should be able to find someone offering such a service by personal recommendation, or by looking through the columns of birdkeeping magazines. It is a good idea to make necessary enquiries in advance, just in case you find yourself in such a situation; for example, if a hen dies suddenly, leaving a clutch of young chicks in the nest that the cock will not feed.

Some breeders use a service of this kind on a regular basis, removing the first clutch of eggs from their parrots for artificial incubation, and having the chicks raised by hand. With their eggs taken away shortly after they were laid, the adult pair will be encouraged to nest again quite rapidly, often within a few weeks. The reproductive potential of a pair

Below: *This young Eclectus Parrot is being hand-fed, using an adapted teaspoon. Special rearing foods are now available for parrot chicks.*

is thus effectively doubled.

If you decide or need to incubate and hand-raise chicks yourself, you will need to start by obtaining a reliable incubator. A number of models now have a proven track record in hatching parrot eggs. Look through various birdkeeping magazines to find precise information on the particular makes available. Forced-air incubators, which rely on a fan to drive the warm air through the unit, are more commonly used than still-air types.

The eggs will need to be turned perhaps six times a day to prevent the embryo becoming stuck to its surrounding shell membranes. It is therefore important to choose a model that incorporates an automatic turning system, so this can be done without you having to open the incubator and thus lose vital heat from the unit.

The temperature needs to be maintained in the range of 36.9–37.5°C(98.5–99.5°F), and you will therefore need a thermometer that can register changes of 0.5°C(1°F). The relative humidity within the incubator should be kept at 40–50%, and this is usually measured using a wet and dry bulb thermometer, which may be supplied with the incubator. You will then need to compare the readings from a set of tables to establish the relative humidity.

Once the chicks hatch, maintain them at the incubation temperature for the first couple of days or so, before gradually reducing the temperature. You will need a separate brooder, in which to rear the chicks. This needs to incorporate an adjustable heat supply, under accurate thermostatic control, and ventilation holes. Transfer the chicks to the new brooder in clean empty margarine containers, lined with tissues, in small groups to help them maintain their body warmth.

Hand-rearing is much more straightforward than it used to be, as there are now specially formulated diets available for this purpose. Previously, breeders were forced to rely on human infant foods, which needed to be diluted with water for feeding chicks. Offer

Below: *Incubating parrot eggs. The temperature in the incubator needs to be kept constant, so do not open the unit more than necessary.*

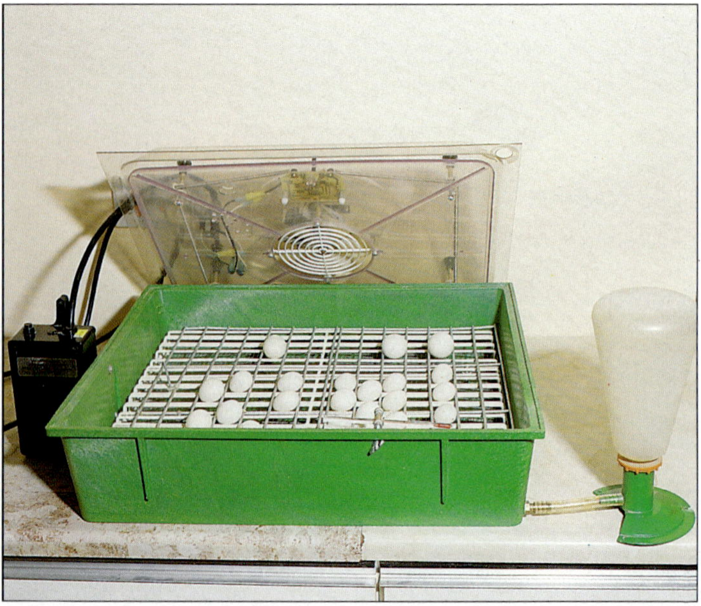

the rearing food, mixing enough for only the one feed, at a temperature not exceeding about 40°C(105°F). Feed the chick in a warm environment, so that it does not become chilled while out of the brooder, using a teaspoon with its sides bent to form a funnel. Allow the chick to feed slowly at its own pace; if you rush this procedure the bird may choke. Always wipe the chick's soft beak tissue after a feed to remove any food deposits before they can harden and cause any malformation.

Keep a close watch on the crop and fill it at each feed. By the time the crop has emptied, the chick will be ready for another meal. It is a good idea to weigh the chicks at the same time each day, so that you can monitor their growth.

As the chicks start to feather up, you can add ground sunflower seed kernels to the feeding mixture. When the time for weaning approaches, offer the chicks seeds, which they may play with and start to crack. At this stage, they will begin to take less interest in the hand-feeding mixture, and will be difficult to feed with a spoon.

Above: *Suitable brooders are not widely marketed at present, and you may need to make one. These Grey Parrot chicks are being reared in a wooden brooder.*

Do not be in a rush to place the chicks in an outside aviary as soon as they are eating independently. They will be used to a warm environment and will need careful acclimatization. If you intend to breed these young birds eventually, you should keep them together to prevent them relating more closely to people than other parrots.

Blue-fronted Amazon

Amazona aestiva

● **Distribution:** Bolivia, Brazil and northern Argentina.
● **Size:** 36cm(14in).
● **Sexing:** Visual distinction between the sexes is not possible.
● **Youngsters:** Duller than adults, with a reduced area of yellow and blue on the head.

One of the most widely kept amazons, the Blue-fronted is now becoming even more popular as an aviary bird than it has long been as a pet. It is known to be one of the longest lived of all parrot species, with a potential lifespan of nearly a century in captivity.

Although colour mutations are rare in New World parrots at present, several brilliant lutino examples of this species have been documented. Such birds are bright yellow, with white markings replacing the usual blue ones.

Below: **Blue-fronted Amazon**
The attractive red wing speculum, shown here, helps to distinguish this species from the Orangewing.

White-fronted Amazon

Amazona albifrons

- **Distribution:** From Mexico to Costa Rica in Central America.
- **Size:** 25cm(10in).
- **Sexing:** Hens usually have green rather than red wing coverts.
- **Youngsters:** Juveniles have less red plumage than adults and a yellowish rather than white area on the head.

This parrot, which is the smallest of the 27 different species of amazon, and less raucous than its larger relatives, is becoming a more common sight in collections than it has been in the past. White-fronted Amazons are easy to sex visually and breeding results are now fairly frequently reported. Three or four eggs form the usual clutch, and the incubation period lasts around 25 days, as for other amazons. The chicks fledge when they are about seven weeks old.

Below: **White-fronted Amazon**
This attractive and relatively quiet amazon is the only member of the genus that can be sexed by sight.

Orange-winged Amazon

Amazona amazonica

● **Distribution:** Over much of northern South America, as well as Trinidad and Tobago.
● **Size:** 30cm(11.75in).
● **Sexing:** Visual distinction between the sexes is not possible.
● **Youngsters:** Resemble adults, but with dark brown rather than orange irides.

This species may be confused with the Blue-fronted Amazon, but is distinguishable from the latter by its smaller size and paler beak. As its name suggests, it also has an orange rather than red wing speculum, and similar orange markings at the base of its tail.

Orangewings are talented mimics, but are also rather noisy. Breeding details are similar to those of the White-fronted Amazon, but there are likely to be only three eggs in an average clutch.

Below: **Orange-winged Amazon** *A popular pet bird, this species is now being bred increasingly in collections. Head markings vary.*

Red-lored Amazon
Amazona autumnalis

● **Distribution:** Central America, from eastern Mexico down to western Ecuador, with an isolated population in northwestern Brazil.
● **Size:** 34cm(13.5in).
● **Sexing:** Visual distinction between the sexes is not possible.
● **Youngsters:** Juveniles have dark irides and their head markings are less colourful than those of adults.

Of the four distinct races recognized, you are likely to see only the two Central American forms; the nominate form and Salvin's Amazon *(A. a. salvini)*. Salvin's Amazon is larger than the nominate race, and lacks the yellow cheek markings of the latter.

More of these amazons have become available to aviculturists in recent years, as export quotas have been established, and breeding results have become more common during the 1980s.

Below: **Red-lored Amazon**
This species is also known as the Primrose-cheeked Amazon.

Mealy Amazon

Amazona farinosa

● **Distribution:** East of the Andes, from southern Mexico, south as far as Bolivia and eastern Brazil.
● **Size:** 38cm(15in).
● **Sexing:** Visual distinction between the sexes is not possible.
● **Youngsters:** Significantly duller than adults, with dark brown irides.

Mealies are large amazons, and rank among the most raucous members of a noisy group. However, they are long lived and, if you buy young birds, they will normally become very tame.

The Central American race *(A. f. guatemalae)* is the most colourful, with an area of blue extending from the top of the head to the nape of the neck, and yellow cheek patches. The nominate race, *A. f. farinosa,* is easily distinguishable, being largely green with an area of yellow on the crown of the head.

Below: **Mealy Amazon**
These large amazons are intelligent, and have lively, if somewhat noisy, natures. Races vary in coloration.

Lilac-crowned Amazon
Amazona finschi

- **Distribution:** Western Mexico.
- **Size:** 33cm(13in).
- **Sexing:** Visual distinction between the sexes is not possible.
- **Youngsters:** Recognizable by their dark irides.

These amazons tend to be more widely kept in North American than in European collections. They are similar in appearance to the Green-cheeked *(A. viridigenalis),* but the area of red on their head is smaller and does not extend over the eyes.

Pairs have nested on various occasions. In common with other amazons, they will rarely start breeding in an outdoor aviary before May in northern temperate regions. Three eggs form the usual clutch and incubation lasts about 26 days. The chicks fledge approximately eight weeks later.

Above: **Lilac-crowned Amazon**
Also sometimes called Finsch's Amazon, this species is not widely available in Europe, although small numbers are bred each year.

Yellow-fronted Amazon

Amazona ochrocephala

● **Distribution:** From Central Mexico to Peru and the Amazon Basin.
● **Size:** 35cm (13.75in).
● **Sexing:** Visual distinction between the sexes is not possible.
● **Youngsters:** Irides are dark and yellow markings are less extensive than those of the adult birds.

There is often confusion over this species, as many different races are recognized, varying largely in the amount of yellow plumage on their heads. The most colourful are the so-called Double yellowhead and its related forms, of which there are four in all. The completely yellow head of mature birds develops with successive moults, taking place over a period of about four years. You are most likely to encounter the yellow-fronted race from Guyana, although, recently, the yellow-naped *(A. o. auropalliata)*, with yellow plumage on the nape of the neck, has become more commonly available. This yellow-naped form of the species is currently being exported on a quota system, like some other Central American amazons, but appears more reluctant to breed in captive collections than other forms of the Yellow-fronted.

Below: **Yellow-fronted Amazon**
Various races of the Yellow-fronted Amazon are found over a wide area, from Central America to Colombia and parts of Brazil. This is the most commonly seen form.

Below right:
Double Yellow-headed Amazon
The more colourful forms of the Yellow-fronted, such as this, are relatively scarce in aviculture, but more are now being bred.

Above: **Tucuman Amazon**
This species is now protected in its homeland, in common with other rarer species of amazon. Their sale will require a licence in many countries. Check with your wildlife department.

Tucuman Amazon
Amazona tucumana

● **Distribution:** Eastern Andes, in southeastern Bolivia and Argentina.
● **Size:** 30cm (11.75in).
● **Sexing:** Visual distinction between the sexes is not possible.
● **Youngsters:** Yellow or orange markings in the red patch above the nostrils, and green thighs.

It appears that this species differs somewhat from other amazons in its lifestyle; it inhabits Alder trees (from which it takes its alternative common name) in the wild. Its beak is relatively thin and pointed, and may be used for extracting seeds – pine nuts are a favourite food. This lively species was only available for a relatively short period in the 1980s. Pairs have proved to be quite keen to nest, so captive-bred birds are now available.

Green-cheeked Amazon
Amazona viridigenalis

● **Distribution:** Northeastern Mexico.
● **Size:** 33cm(13in).
● **Sexing:** Visual distinction between the sexes is not possible.
● **Youngsters:** The red area on the forehead is smaller than on adults, and young birds have dark irides.

Sometimes known as Mexican Red-headed Amazons, these parrots were quite often available during the 1970s, and a number of pairs are now established in collections. Like other amazons, they will frequently flare their tail feathers when in breeding condition, creating a momentary fanlike effect. The pupils of their eyes may also constrict, causing the eye to appear more colourful. This is sometimes described as 'eye blazing'. Breeding details do not differ significantly from those of other members of the genus. The hen stays in the nestbox for at least three weeks after the chicks hatch. She will then begin to leave the nest for progressively longer periods during the day, but will return to brood the chicks at night until they are about five or six weeks old.

Below: **Green-cheeked Amazon**
A species more commonly kept in North America than in Europe. Pairs usually nest quite readily.

Blue and Gold Macaw

Ara ararauna

● **Distribution:** From eastern Panama across most of northern South America, except western coastal areas, extending to Bolivia, Paraguay and Brazil.
● **Size:** 86cm(34in).
● **Sexing:** Visual distinction between the sexes is not normally possible, although hens may have narrower heads than the cocks.
● **Youngsters:** Young birds have dark irides.

In spite of their large beaks, these birds can be extremely gentle once tame. Nevertheless, be cautious when handling an unfamiliar macaw, as these birds can inflict a very painful bite. An aviary for these macaws needs to be suitably robust, and will be expensive to construct. Bear in mind, too, that macaws can be noisy, especially when in breeding condition. The usual clutch consists of two or three eggs, which hatch after about 28 days. The young macaws then spend a further three months or so in the nest. A rare mutation of this species, in which the yellow pigment is absent, creating a blue and white bird, has been reported.

Below: **Blue and Gold Macaw**
An impressive, but rather noisy species. Providing accommodation for these large birds is costly.

Yellow-collared Macaw
Ara auricollis

● **Distribution:** From Matto Grosso, Brazil, to Bolivia, Paraguay and parts of northwestern Argentina.
● **Size:** 38cm(15in).
● **Sexing:** Visual distinction between the sexes is not possible.
● **Youngsters:** Easily recognizable by their grey rather than pink feet.

This is one of the smaller, predominantly green species, sometimes referred to collectively as the dwarf macaws. These birds are usually easier to house and maintain, especially in an urban locality, than the larger multi-coloured species. Pairs will normally nest quite readily, with the hen laying up to three eggs in a clutch. Incubation lasts 25 days, and the chicks fledge at about nine weeks old. Hand-raised birds of this species make very tame pets, and often start talking soon after they become independent.

Below: **Yellow-collared Macaw**
This species is instantly recognizable by its yellow collar.

Green-winged Macaw
Ara chloroptera

● **Distribution:** From eastern Panama in Central America, south across most of northern South America, east of the Andes, to Bolivia, Brazil and Paraguay.
● **Size:** 90cm(35.5in).
● **Sexing:** Visual distinction between the sexes is not normally possible, but some cocks may have broader heads than the hens.
● **Youngsters:** Recognizable by their dark irides.

These majestic birds are very similar to Blue and Gold Macaws in their requirements. Pairs can usually be persuaded to nest, but young birds breeding for the first time may prove unreliable parents when feeding their chicks. Avoid disturbing the birds if all appears to be progressing well, and provide plenty of greenfood, such as spinach beet, vegetables, such as corn-on-the-cob and carrot, and fruit laced with a food supplement as rearing foods. This will help to ensure that the chicks do not develop any skeletal abnormalities during the relatively long period they spend in the nestbox before they emerge at about 13 weeks old.

Above: **Green-winged Macaw**
This large species needs plenty of space, but tame birds can become very devoted to their owners.

Scarlet Macaw
Ara macao

● **Distribution:** From eastern Panama in Central America, south across most of northern South America, east of the Andes, as far as parts of Bolivia, Paraguay and Brazil.
● **Size:** 85cm(33.5in).
● **Sexing:** Visual distinction between the sexes is not normally possible, but some cocks may have broader heads than the hens.
● **Youngsters:** Juveniles have brown irides.

This species, also known as the Red and Gold Macaw, can be easily recognized by the characteristic area of yellow plumage on its wings, which helps to distinguish it from the Greenwing (also known as the Red and Green Macaw). The Scarlet Macaw has declined in numbers in the northern part of its very wide range because of deforestation. As a result, it has been listed as an endangered species, which means that you may need to apply for a permit when selling, purchasing or moving these macaws. Contact your national CITES Management Authority for advice about the current position.

Below: **Scarlet Macaw**
A striking, but rare, species. Keep pairs of these large macaws on their own to prevent hybridization.

Red-bellied Macaw
Ara manilata

- **Distribution:** Over much of northern South America to Peru and parts of Brazil.
- **Size:** 48cm(19in).
- **Sexing:** Visual distinction between the sexes is not possible.
- **Youngsters:** Have dark irides.

The management of this species has proved rather difficult in the past. The Red-bellied is less hardy than other macaws after being acclimatized, and may need to be transferred indoors for the winter period. It has also acquired a reputation for having a nervous disposition, and birds sometimes die unexpectedly. Further study has shown that these macaws rapidly become obese, and this, apparently, has been responsible for the premature death of individuals. You can prevent obesity by ensuring that a high proportion of fruit and vegetables forms part of their regular diet, and by placing a greater emphasis on cereal seeds, such as corn-on-the-cob, maize and millet sprays in their diet, than on oil-rich sunflower seed. In spite of their wide distribution, these macaws have been generally available to aviculturists only since the mid 1980s. Now, with better insight into the dietary needs of these birds, breeders are starting to obtain positive results.

Above: **Red-bellied Macaw**
Less robust than other macaws, these birds are prone to obesity.

Hahn's Macaw
Ara nobilis

● **Distribution:** North of the Amazon, from Venezuela to northeastern Brazil.
● **Size:** 30cm(11.75in).
● **Sexing:** Visual distinction between the sexes is not possible.
● **Youngsters:** Recognizable by the lack of red on their wing edges, and the reduced area of blue plumage on the head.

This species is the smallest of the macaws, but is instantly recognizable as belonging to this group of parrots by the bare patches of skin on the sides of its face. As with the larger species, these may become redder if the bird becomes excited, because of increased blood flow.

Above: **Hahn's Macaw**
This species is the smallest of the macaw family. Note the prominent area of bare skin on the face, which is characteristic of the group.

Unlike many parrots, Hahn's Macaws are sociable, even when breeding. You can keep pairs together in a colony, and they will nest readily in such surroundings, without aggression in most cases. Nestboxes measuring 23cm(9in) square and 46cm(18in) deep will suit them well. They are often prolific, with hens laying a clutch of as many as five eggs, which should hatch after an incubation period of 25 days. The chicks leave the nest at two months old. Hand-reared Hahn's Macaws make ideal pets; they will become very tame and are easy to manage.

Severe Macaw

Ara severa

● **Distribution:** From eastern Panama in Central America, south as far as Bolivia and Brazil.
● **Size:** 51cm(20in).
● **Sexing:** Visual distinction between the sexes is not possible.
● **Youngsters:** Have dark irides.

Occuring over a wide area, the Severe Macaw, also known as the Chestnut-fronted, has never been very popular, possibly because of its rather plain coloration.

A nestbox measuring 30cm(12in) square and about 77cm(30in) high will be suitable for a breeding pair. Two or three eggs form the usual clutch, with the incubation period lasting 28 days. The young fledge at about nine weeks old. If you have a compatible pair, you should obtain consistently good results from this and other macaw species over many years.

Below: **Severe Macaw**
The green coloration of these so-called dwarf macaws takes on an attractive sheen in the sunlight.

Hawk-headed Parrot

Deroptyus accipitrinus

● **Distribution:** Northern Brazil and the Guianas to southeastern Colombia and northeastern Peru.
● **Size:** 30cm(11.75in).
● **Sexing:** Visual distinction between the sexes is not possible.
● **Youngsters:** Juveniles have brown irides and a green crown.

Undoubtedly the most bizarre of all parrots, the Hawkhead has a ruff of feathers around its neck, which it raises when excited or alarmed. This behaviour is accompanied by hissing and swaying and it seems likely that it has originated as a deterrent to predators.

In some ways, the Hawkhead appears more closely related to the *Pyrrhura* conures than to other parrots of similar size. Bear in mind, however, that Hawkheads can prove exceptionally noisy birds and that they need a significant amount of fruit and other fresh foods as part of their regular diet.

Breeding is difficult, and hand-rearing, although often advised because of the nervous nature of these parrots, is itself often fraught with problems. The hen lays two or three eggs, which she incubates for about 28 days. The chicks should fledge about nine weeks later.

Below: **Hawk-headed Parrot**
This species' magnificent ruff, displayed here, is raised when the parrot is excited or alarmed.

Celestial Parrotlet
Forpus coelestis

● **Distribution:** Ecuador and Peru.
● **Size:** 14cm(5.5in).
● **Sexing:** Hens are mainly green, lacking the blue markings of cocks, although they may have a bluish tinge on their rumps.
● **Youngsters:** Resemble adults, but are duller overall.

This group of small birds will often breed quite readily and will offer you an ideal opportunity to specialize in developing strains, even if your budget and surroundings are rather limited. Results tend to be better in small aviaries than in cages, as some cocks can prove very aggressive towards their offspring as the time for fledging approaches, and may even cause fatalities. Ideally, you should remove the chicks as soon as they are independent, not only to protect them, but because the adult birds may well be nesting again. The hen may lay six or seven eggs in a clutch and the chicks will be mature by the following breeding season. Offer reasonable amounts of greenfood, along with millet sprays, during the rearing period. This species is also sometimes known as the Pacific Parrotlet.

Below: **Celestial Parrotlets**
The bright blue markings are clearly displayed in the cock of this attractive pair. The hen, on the lower branch, is much duller.

Green-rumped Parrotlet

Forpus passerinus

● **Distribution:** From Colombia and Venezuela, east to the Guianas and northern Brazil.
● **Size:** 12.5cm(5in).
● **Sexing:** Hens have yellowish heads and lack the blue plumage of the cock birds.
● **Youngsters:** Similar to adults.

As with other *Forpus* species, it is much safer to house these birds in individual pairs, than to attempt to keep them on a colony basis. The incubation period lasts about 18 days, and the chicks leave the nest approximately six weeks later. In spite of their small size, parrotlets are relatively hardy, providing they are properly acclimatized, and can have a long reproductive life of 15 years or more. They may choose to roost in a nestbox at night, rather than on a perch, and you should encourage this behaviour during cold weather. Transfer the nestbox to the shelter for extra protection.

Above: **Green-rumped Parrotlet**
An easy species to cater for. Note the striking blue plumage under the wings of this cock bird.

Yellow-faced Parrotlet
Forpus xanthops

● **Distribution:** A small area of northwestern Peru.
● **Size:** 14.5cm(5.75in).
● **Sexing:** Hens have a pale blue rather than violet rump.
● **Youngsters:** Duller than adults, with a dark stripe on the beak.

A small number of these parrotlets were first imported from Peru in 1979 and were available for several years. Although they have since been scarce, some breeders are successfully developing their own strains from this original stock. The Yellow-faced Parrotlet is similar to the Celestial, but has lighter coloration. These birds were difficult to establish initially because of *microfilariae* (immature parasitic worms) present in the circulatory system and avian malaria. These parasites caused sudden losses of birds that otherwise appeared healthy. Such problems are unlikely to arise with captive-bred stock, however.

Below: **Yellow-faced Parrotlets** *The cock (shown left) has brighter coloration than the hen. Although still scarce, these parrotlets are now being bred in larger numbers.*

White-bellied Caique
Pionites leucogaster

● **Distribution:** South of the Amazon, from northern Brazil to parts of Bolivia, Peru and Ecuador.
● **Size:** 23cm(9in).
● **Sexing:** Visual distinction between the sexes is not possible.
● **Youngsters:** Juveniles have brown irides and some black feathers on the head.

These attractive parrots are surprisingly destructive for their size and can be quite noisy. On the positive side, however, they often become very tame, even in aviary surroundings. Caiques are highly social birds, so keep them in pairs rather than on their own. They also have a long lifespan – a number have lived for at least 40 years.

Below: **White-bellied Caique**
This species tends to be less often seen than its black-headed relative. The two are similar in their habits. Pairs often nest more readily when their nestbox is in a secluded spot.

Black-headed Caique
Pionites melanocephala

● **Distribution:** North of the Amazon, in the Guianas, and westwards to parts of Colombia, Venezuela, Ecuador and Peru.
● **Size:** 23cm(9in).
● **Sexing:** Visual distinction between the sexes is not possible.
● **Youngsters:** Juveniles have brown irides and horn-coloured rather than black beaks.

This species is very similar to the White-bellied Caique in its habits.

Above: **Black-headed Caique**
These birds are often very playful, but individuals may turn vicious when first introduced to each other.

Supply these birds with plenty of fresh perches to gnaw so that their beaks do not become overgrown. You can encourage pairs to nest by providing them with a nestbox in a dark locality. The hen will lay up to four eggs and these should hatch after 25 days. Offer plenty of fruit as part of their diet, along with an occasional treat of walnuts, which are favourites of most caiques.

Bronze-winged Pionus

Pionus chalcopterus

● **Distribution:** Mountainous parts of Venezuela, Colombia, Ecuador and Peru.
● **Size:** 28cm(11in).
● **Sexing:** Visual distinction between the sexes is not possible.
● **Youngsters:** Juveniles have yellowish rather than grey skin around the eyes.

The pionus are a group of seven medium-sized parrots that, although not brightly coloured, have attractive hues in their plumage. Bronzewings show to best effect in an outside aviary where the bright blue coloration under their wings will be visible when the birds are in flight.

The pair bond tends to be quite strong, and over-enthusiastic preening may result in the birds plucking each other around the back of the neck. Because pionus parrots are rather nervous by nature, breeding can be difficult.

Below: **Bronze-winged Pionus**
The subtle coloration of this species is best seen when the birds are housed in an outdoor aviary.

Dusky Pionus

Pionus fuscus

● **Distribution:** From Colombia through Venezuela, the Guianas and Brazil, north of the Amazon.
● **Size:** 24cm(9.5in).
● **Sexing:** Visual distinction between the sexes is not possible.
● **Youngsters:** Juveniles have a greenish tinge over their wings.

This is one of the less commonly available pionus species, and shows considerable variation in its coloration. If possible, try to obtain young birds, which will settle well and should prove less nervous than adults. Unfortunately, there seems to be a preponderance of hens in this species, and you may have difficulty in obtaining a cock bird. Although they have been hybridized with other pionus species, this practice is not recommended, and any offspring resulting from hybridization should be sold as pets.

Below: **Dusky Pionus**
Individuals of this unusually coloured species may vary slightly in their markings, but this is not a reliable sign of sexual dimorphism.

Maximilian's Parrot

Pionus maximiliana

● **Distribution:** Over much of eastern South America, from northern Brazil to Bolivia, Paraguay and Argentina.
● **Size:** 30cm(11.75in).
● **Sexing:** Visual distinction between the sexes is not possible.
● **Youngsters:** May have less blue in their upper breasts than adults.

Also known as the Scaly headed Parrot, this species is one of the most widely kept members of the genus and has now been bred on a number of occasions. Pairs may take mealworms when they have chicks in the nest and greenfood is also a popular rearing food. The hen lays up to five eggs, which she incubates for 26 days, and the young leave the nest by the time they are eight weeks old.

Below: **Maximilian's Parrot**
Reasonably quiet and easy to maintain in an aviary, this species is becoming increasingly popular.

Blue-headed Pionus
Pionus menstruus

● **Distribution:** From southern Costa Rica in Central America, through South America to parts of Bolivia and central Brazil.
● **Size:** 28cm(11in).
● **Sexing:** Visual distinction between the sexes is not possible.
● **Youngsters:** Mainly green in colour and duller than adults.

The coloration of these pionus parrots is quite variable, some birds having a darker shade of blue on their heads than others. The amount of pink under the chin also varies.

Hand-raised chicks of this species should develop into delightful pets, and are far less noisy than most amazons. Adult birds, once properly acclimatized, can be kept in outside aviaries throughout the year. Position a nestbox in a darkened area to encourage breeding activity. Reproductive details are similar to those of Maximilian's Parrot.

Above: **Blue-headed Pionus**
If you obtain a juvenile of this attractive species, it may become quite tame and even learn to talk.

White-crowned Pionus
Pionus senilis

● **Distribution:** Central America, from southwestern Mexico to western Panama.
● **Size:** 24cm(9.5in).
● **Sexing:** Visual distinction between the sexes is not possible.
● **Youngsters:** The area around the eyes is grey rather than red.

These parrots are becoming more easily obtainable, and successful breeding results are recorded with increasing frequency. Corn-on-the-cob is a favoured rearing food and is worth growing in your garden if you have space.

When purchasing pionus parrots, pay particular attention to their breathing. Although they may breathe noisily when you approach them – a normal reaction to stress – they also seem more vulnerable to aspergillosis (see page 46) than some other species.

Above: **White-crowned Pionus**
Like other pionus parrots, this species (also sometimes known as the White-capped Parrot) is not very noisy. Surgical sexing is necessary to distinguish true pairs.

Lesser Vasa Parrot

Coracopsis nigra

● **Distribution:** Madagascar and neighbouring islands.
● **Size:** 35cm(13.75in).
● **Sexing:** A large protuberance from the vent is clearly visible in cocks in breeding condition.
● **Youngsters:** Similar to adults, but with a lighter bill.

Although these highly unusual parrots lack the bright coloration of some species, they make fascinating aviary occupants. Some birds are afflicted with sporadic white feathering in their plumage, which may increase or regress at subsequent moults and probably corresponds to the patchy yellow feathers that are sometimes present in Blue-fronted Amazons. A varied diet and suitable food supplements may help to overcome this problem.

It is easy to detect the onset of the breeding period, when a large protuberance from the male's vent is clearly visible. (This prolapse is no cause for concern.) Two or three eggs form the usual clutch.

The Greater Vasa *(C. vasa)* is similar in its habits, but prefers more seeds in its diet than the Lesser Vasa – an avid fruit-eater. The Greater is also more vocal, and about 15cm(6in) larger.

Above: **Lesser Vasa Parrot**
This distinctive species was rarely seen in collections until the early 1980s, but pairs have since been bred on various occasions.

Left: **Greater Vasa Parrot**
The rather noisy Greater Vasa is distinguishable from the Lesser by its larger size and the more pinkish coloration of its legs.

Jardine's Parrot

Poicephalus gulielmi

● **Distribution:** Western and central Africa.
● **Size:** 28cm(11in).
● **Sexing:** Hens may have brown irides, whereas those of cocks are reddish brown.
● **Youngsters:** Much duller, lacking the orange markings of adult birds.

This is one of the larger *Poicephalus* species and is less regularly available than either the Senegal or Meyer's. Its coloration is variable; birds originating from the Cameroon tend to be a deeper shade of fiery orange than those found further east.

The breeding display of these birds includes tail-flaring. The hen usually lays four eggs, which she incubates alone for about 26 days.

Right: **Jardine's Parrot**
The depth and extent of the orange markings vary between individuals.

Left: **Meyer's Parrot**
These colouful parrots are quite hardy once properly acclimatized.

Meyer's Parrot
Poicephalus meyeri

● **Distribution:** Central and eastern parts of Africa.
● **Size:** 20cm(8in).
● **Sexing:** Visual distinction between the sexes is not possible.
● **Youngsters:** Generally duller in coloration than adults.

Although Meyer's Parrots may vary noticeably in their markings, this is not a sign of sexual dimorphism; because the species occurs over such a wide area, at least six distinctive races have evolved. These parrots are attractive aviary birds, although they may prove rather shy. Unlike many other parrots, they are not noisy, and are therefore ideal occupants for an aviary in fairly urbanized surroundings. Hand-reared chicks can develop into very tame pets, and may learn to say a few words.

Senegal Parrot

Poicephalus senegalus

● **Distribution:** Western and central Africa, further north than Jardine's Parrot (see page 88).
● **Size:** 23cm(9in).
● **Sexing:** Visual distinction between the sexes is not possible.
● **Youngsters:** Duller than adults with dark irides.

The most commonly seen of the *Poicephalus* parrots, the Senegal is an easy species to maintain in good health. Its call is inoffensive, but its powerful beak needs an adequate supply of perches to divert its attention from the aviary woodwork, especially at the onset of the breeding period.

Breeding details are similar to those of Jardine's Parrot, with the chicks fledging at just over nine weeks old. However, breeding results tend to be harder to obtain than for other members of the genus. Pairs often prefer to nest quite early in the year, which reduces the likelihood of successful breeding during cold weather. Place their nestbox in a dark locality, such as the shelter.

Below: **Senegal Parrot**
These parrots are ideal for the smaller garden aviary. Their calls are comprised largely of whistles.

Grey Parrot
Psittacus erithacus

● **Distribution:** Over a broad band of central Africa.
● **Size:** 33cm(13in).
● **Sexing:** Cocks sometimes have a darker back and wings than hens.
● **Youngsters:** Recognizable by their dark irides.

These parrots have been kept as pets for centuries, but are now being bred in much greater numbers. If you want to keep them as aviary birds, you will need to take particular care with their acclimatization. The Timneh subspecies *(P. e. timneh)* – from Sierra Leone and parts of Guinea, the Ivory Coast and Liberia – can be easily distinguished from the more common nominate race by its maroon rather than scarlet tail feathers. It is also slightly smaller and invariably less costly. Both races are talented mimics.

Adult Greys can prove nervous birds and may take several years to adapt to new surroundings before they start to breed. Hens generally lay three or four eggs in a clutch, and incubation lasts four weeks. Provide a good varied diet, especially during the rearing period. The chicks should leave the nest at about three months old and will soon be feeding independently. The pair bond in this species is very strong, and the birds will show great devotion to each other.

Above: **Grey Parrot**
Probably the best loved of all pet parrots, the Grey is also acknowledged as a talented mimic.

Eclectus Parrot
Eclectus roratus

● **Distribution:** Islands of eastern Indonesia and New Guinea.
● **Size:** 35cm(13.75in).
● **Sexing:** Even chicks are clearly dimorphic; cocks are mainly green and hens red.
● **Youngsters:** Similar to adults, but with brown irides.

Occurring over many islands, the Eclectus Parrot has evolved into at least ten different races. Although the appearance of hens tends to be similar, cocks may vary quite widely in their markings depending on their distribution. Fruit and greenstuff are essential to keep these birds in good health. They have a long digestive tract, adapted to a fibrous diet, and if deprived of such foods, may rapidly succumb to candidiasis.

Pairs are normally keen to nest, although some hens can prove spiteful towards intended mates. Two eggs form the usual clutch, and hatch after about 28 days. You can encourage egg laying by separating a pair and then placing them, together, in breeding quarters about three weeks later. Avoid over-breeding, or soft-shelled eggs and egg-binding may result. Supplement the diet of breeding birds with plenty of cuttlefish bone, as their chicks can be prone to rickets.

The main drawback of the Eclectus as an aviary bird is its loud calls. Nevertheless, the species is well established in aviculture.

Below: **Eclectus Parrot**
These parrots can be very easily sexed; this cock bird is distinguishable from the red hen by its predominantly green plumage.

Great-billed Parrot
Tanygnathus megalorhynchos

- **Distribution:** Indonesia, and Balut in the Philippines.
- **Size:** 41cm(16in).
- **Sexing:** Difficult to sex visually, but cocks may have larger beaks and brighter coloration than hens.
- **Youngsters:** Similar to adults, but lacking black on the wings.

The requirements of these parrots are similar to those of the Eclectus but, unlike the latter, Greatbills are not continuous nesters, normally laying only two or three eggs during a breeding season. Incubation lasts about 30 days.

Above: **Great-billed Parrot**
This species needs careful acclimatization, and plenty of fruit, greenstuff and carrot in its diet.

Great-billed Parrots can become quite tame and, although not common in aviculture, they make interesting aviary occupants. Their calls, while loud, are not normally persistent, but these birds require a solidly constructed aviary because of their destructive natures.

Index of species

Page numbers in **bold** indicate major references including accompanying photographs. Page numbers in *italics* indicate captions to other illustrations. Less important text entries are shown in normal type.

A

Amazona aestiva **60**
A. albifrons **61**
A. amazonica **62**
A. autumnalis **63**
A. a. salvini 63
A. farinosa **64**
A. f. farinosa 64
A. f. guatemalae 64
A. finschi **65**
A. ochrocephala **66**
A. o. auropalliata 66
A. tucumana **67**
A. viridigenalis 65, **68**
Amazons 9, 13, *14*, 15, 16, 21, 26, 33, 37, 39, 40, 46, 47, 54, 56, 60, 61, 63, 64, 65, 67, 68, 85
Ara ararauna **69**
A. auricollis **70**
A. chloroptera **71**
A. macao **72**
*A. manilata***73**
A. nobilis **74**
A. severa **75**

B

Black-headed Caique *Contents page, 80* **81**
Blue and Gold Macaw *36,* **69**, 71
Blue-fronted Amazon **60**, 87
lutino 60
Blue-headed Pionus **85**
Bronze-winged Pionus **82**

C

Caiques 80
Celestial Parrotlet *Contents page,* **77**, 79
Chestnut-fronted Macaw *See* Severe Macaw
Coracopsis nigra **87**
C. vasa 87

D

Deroptyus accipitrinus **76**
Double Yellow-headed Amazon 13, 66, *66*
Dusky Pionus **83**
Dwarf macaws 70

E

Eclectus Parrot *11*, 11, 14, 15, 39, 41, 46, 50, *57,* **92**
E. roratus 92

F

Finsch's Amazon *See* Lilac-crowned Amazon
Forpus 78
F. coelestis **77**
F. passerinus **78**
F. xanthops **79**

G

Great-billed Parrot 14, 15, 39, 46, **93**
Greater Vasa Parrot 87, *87*
Green-cheeked Amazon *10,* 65, **68**
Green-rumped Parrotlet **78**
Green-winged Macaw *Title page, 54,* **71**
Grey Parrot 7, *8*, 11, 13, 15, 23, 24, *24*, 31, 33, 39, 47, 54, *59,* **91**

H

Hahn's Macaw **74**
Hawk-headed Parrot **76**

J

Jardine's Parrot *42,* **88**, 90

L

Lesser Vasa Parrot **87**
Lilac-crowned Amazon **65**

M

Macaws 6, 7, 8, *13*, 13, 15, 16, *16*, 19, 22, 23, 24, 26, *27*, 30, 33, 35, 36, 37, 39, 40, 47, 50, *52, 53,* 54, 55, 56, 69, 73, 74
Maximilian's Parrot **84**, 85
Mealy Amazon **64**
Mexican Red-headed Amazon *See* Green-cheeked Amazon
Meyer's Parrot 88, **89**

O

Orange-winged Amazon *60,* **62**

P

Pacific Parrotlet *See* Celestial Parrotlet
Parrotlets 9, 15, 16, 19, 23, 26, *27*, 28, *28*, 32, 37, 38, 39, 43, 48, 79
Pionites leucogaster **80**
P. melanocephala **81**
Pionus 15, 23, 26, 39, 54, 82, 83, 85, 86
P. chalcopterus **82**
P. fuscus **83**
P. maximiliana **84**
P. menstruus **85**
P. senilis **86**
Poicephalus 15, 23, 33, 37, 39, 54, 55, 88
P. gulielmi **88**
P. meyeri **89**
P. senegalus **90**
Primrose-cheeked Amazon *See* Red-lored Amazon
Psittacus erithacus **91**
P. e. timneh 91

R

Red and Green Macaw *See* Green-winged Macaw
Red and Gold Macaw *See* Scarlet Macaw
Red-bellied Macaw **73**
Red-fronted Macaw *32*
Red-lored Amazon **63**

S

Salvin's Amazon 63
Scaly headed Parrot *See* Maximilian's Parrot
Scarlet Macaw **72**
Senegal Parrot 26, 36, 88, **90**
Severe Macaw **75**

T

Tanygnathus 46
T. megalorhynchos **93**
Tucuman Amazon **67**

V

Vasa parrots 15, 39